Our Perthshire Folk

Stories of Eighteen Local Heroes and One Villain (Maybe!)

Ken Bruce

DEDICATION

Tae aw mah mukkers wha hae pat up wi' me.

Tae aw mah mukkers wha hae helpit me thro' the mirksum years.

To Tippermuir Books and Paul Philippou who have supported my writing journey, without them, these amazing stories may have never been told.

Contents

1 Henry Anselm de Freitas

Of all the war graves I have visited during my research of Perthshire's aviators, the grave of Henry Anselm de Freitas, AFM is the one that I revisit as often as I can. Henry is buried so very far away from his home and was in my view enshrined here, with great love and respect by his wife and her family. Henry is buried in Wellshill Cemetery in Perth, in a Commonwealth War Graves Commission grave, Section O, nearer to the Rannoch Road, close to the cemetery's war memorial. This is the story of how Henry came to be buried in Perth, 4,500 miles away from his home.

Henry Anselm de Freitas was one of 8 children born on 21 April 1917 in Trinidad, West Indies, to Alderman, Henry Alexander de Freitas MBE and Jessimina de Freitas of Port of Spain. During World War Two, 5 of their children served and 3 sons would be lost.

Henry was, by all accounts, an intelligent, charismatic and active boy. He attended a prominent Roman Catholic School, St Mary's College and was awarded the Jerningham Medal for being the top student in the Island Scholarship examinations. Henry left Trinidad in 1935 to attend the Royal School of Mines at London University. Henry did well, he was President of the School of Mines Student Union, Captain of their rowing club and President of the Imperial College Riding Club. As a talented oarsman he represented the Thames Rowing Club at the 1939 Belgian International Regatta in Dinant, Belgium.

Henry de Freitas demonstrated both his humanity and bravery when in June 1937 he dived into the River Thames, near Putney, and successfully saved the life of 11-year-old Cyril Basil Smith who had got into difficulties and was being carried away by a strong ebb tide. He also saved 16-year-old typist, Margaret Bunker who had attempted to first rescue Smith.

Just before the Second World War started, Henry was awarded a scholarship for the 1939-1940 school year to study Petroleum Engineering at the University of Birmingham. He instead joined the RAF, and we know that on 1 July 1940, Leading Aircraftman "Henry Anslem de FREITAS (81695) was granted a commission for the duration of hostilities as Acting Pilot Officer on Probation". By 3 November 1940 he was promoted to Pilot Officer on Probation. For some unknown reason on 20 June 1941 his commission as an officer was terminated, he did however continue flying as a Sergeant and in July of 1943 was awarded the Air Force Medal. Reportedly the first West Indian to be so honoured. Henry became a flying instructor at the Flight Leaders' School with No. 59 Operational Training Unit (O.T.U.), indicating that he was a very skilled pilot.

Henry married Helen Begg of Charles Street, Perth, in September 1941, they could have met while were both students at university in London and possibly when Henry was undertaking flying training in Scotland. The couple produced 2 children, Alexandra Jaqueline and Henry Anselm.

During 1943, De Freitas was serving as a Flight Sergeant, RAFVR (RAF Volunteer Reserve) 1393818 with

RAF No. 59 Squadron OTU (Operational Training Unit). De Freitas was killed, aged just 26, in a training accident when his Canadian built, Hawker Hurricane Mk X (AG111, HK-G) crashed at 15:00 hours on 5 May 1943. De Freitas is reported as crashed onto Horton Moor near Doddington, Northumberland, just north of Wooler. His aircraft crashed after colliding with a Supermarine Spitfire IIA P7902 over Wooler and crashed into a bog close to a dry-stone wall at Doddington Hill. The Spitfire was piloted by Sergeant F.T.L. Futon, RNAZ 416496, aged 19 he was also killed.

The accident happened after a flight of Hurricanes from 59 OTU 'bounced' from above, a formation of Spitfires from 57 OTU in a mock combat attack. De Freitas's Hurricane AG111 had earlier been passed from No. 59 OTU RAF (at RAF Turnhouse) to No. 57 OTU RAF at RAF Eshott, Northumberland, primarily a Spitfire-equipped unit and used Huricane's in a support role. Henry was still listed as from No. 59 OTU at the time of the accident. RAF Eshott during WW2 was the home for between 77 and 100 Mk1 & Mk2 Spitfires, pilots received about 60 hours combat training. No 57 OTU was established there in November 1942. De Freitas I believe may have been instructing on courses at RAF Eshott and RAF Milfield at the time of the accident.

Notes:

Notably, De Freitas's Hurricane is not listed as a Specialised Low Attack Instructors' School (SLAIS) allocated aircraft which was based at RAF Milfield. The Imperial War Museum picture of Hurricane AG111 (Source: © IWM (CH 9222) shows his aircraft on the ground at RAF Milfield, and it bears the unit codes of the Fighter Leaders School based at Charmy Down, Wiltshire. I believe that unknown pilot in the picture is in fact Henry Anselm de Freitas.

RAF Millfield was located just northwest of Wooler in Northumbria, it was chosen as the base for a new unit, designated No. 1 Specialised Low Attack Instructors' School (SLAIS). It was formed there on 7 December 1942, operating until 26 January 1944 when it was absorbed into the Fighter Leaders School. The unit was to provide ground attack practice for pilots from operational squadron based elsewhere. Goswick Sands, about 15 miles to the east, was the location of the ground attack range. It was, however, common for pilots as it looks like in Henry's case to bring with them their personal mount.

De Freitas's Hurricane AG111 was one of a batch of 140 Canadian built Mk. 1 Hurricanes produced at the Fort William (Thunder Bay) plant, arriving in the UK from June 1940. They were built by Canadian Car & Foundry and when powered by a 1,300 horsepower (969 kilowatts) Packard Merlin 28 engine, they were redesignated the Mk. X Hurricane. They were initially fitted with 8 Browning.303 machine guns, later Mk. X variants had 12 guns. If used for ground attack would have been fitted with 2 Vickers Class 'S' 40 mm cannons. Later, aircraft were fitted with 8 unguided 60 pounder RP-3 rockets.

This all happened at a time in 1943 when the intensive training of pilots was possible. The Luftwaffe had turned their attention away to attacking the Soviet Union, 22 June 1941 and the United States were now in the war following the day of infamy attack by the Japanese on Pearl Harbour, 7 December 1941. The other units in that Northumberland area were ground attack training with the new Hawker Typhoon and USAF P-47 Thunderbolts.

Unfortunately, the RAF records for 57 & 59 Operational Training Unit have either not been digitised or are missing. I might one day to need to visit the National Archives in Kew, London to see if they can let me examine them. I am confident that Henry was an excellent pilot and involved in brave action at some point.

The Air Ministry announced on 2 April 1943 the award of the AFM to De Freitas – the first West Indian to be awarded the AFM:

"ROYAL AIR FORCE. The KING has been graciously pleased to approve the following awards: Air Force Medal to Sergeant Henry Anselm de FREITAS."

(The AFM was a military decoration, awarded to personnel of the Royal Air Force and other British Armed Forces, and formerly to personnel of other Commonwealth countries, below commissioned rank, for 'an act or acts of valour, courage or devotion to duty whilst flying, though not in active operations against the enemy.)

De Freitas is commemorated on a memorial to honour those who served and died at RAF Milfield between 1941 and 1946. The memorial was unveiled in 2002 and is located outside the Borders Gliding Club.

After his death, Henry's parents arranged for De Freitas's wife Helen, and their children relocated to Trinidad. Helen lived in Trinidad for 38 years and died in Nashville, Tennessee in 1998. Helen's older sister Jessie, who died in 1941 is buried with Henry in Wellshill Cemetery. I have been unable to find any of Helen's relatives, but I am in contact with Henry's family in Trinidad.

Hurricane Mark X, AG111 HK-G, of No. 59 Operational Training Unit, on the ground at Milfield Hurricane Mark X, AG111 HK-G, of No. 59 Operational Training Unit © IWM (CH 9222), Northumberland (Henry's personal mount)

2 Flight Lieutenant William Reid VC

William Reid was born in Baillieston in Glasgow on 21 December 1921, the son of a blacksmith. He attended Swinton Primary and Coatbridge Secondary School. After training with the RAF in Canada, Reid gained his wings and was commissioned on 19 June 1942 as a pilot officer on probation in the RAF Volunteer Reserve (RAFVR). At RAF Little Rissington, west of Cheltenham, he trained on twin-engined Airspeed Oxfords. Moving on to the Operational Training Unit (OTU) No. 29 at RAF North Luffenham, he was selected as an instructor flying Vickers Wellingtons. He was promoted to flying officer on 19 December 1942.

His first operational mission was with RAF 1654 Conversion Unit at RAF Wigsley, he flew as second pilot in an Avro Lancaster belonging to RAF 9 Squadron to bomb Mönchengladbach. In September 1943, he was posted to RAF 61 Squadron at RAF Syerston where he flew seven sorties attacking various German cities, before his famous raid on Düsseldorf.

At the age of 22 Reid was awarded the Victoria Cross following a raid on Düsseldorf on 3 November 1943: the front of his cockpit was shot away just after crossing the Dutch coast. He was injured in the head, shoulders, and hands, in a fight with a Messerschmitt BF 110. The rear gunner could not fire as the heating circuit had failed and his hands were too cold to press the trigger or operate his microphone to give warning. After a short delay he managed to return fire and the Messerschmitt was driven off.

A second fighter then attacked his RAF 51 Squadron Avro Lancaster, *'O for Oboe'*, the navigator was killed, the wireless operator was fatally wounded, and the flight engineer although injured in the arm gave Reid oxygen and assistance. The rear turret was badly damaged, the communications system and the compasses were put out of action. The windscreen was shattered, and blood was flowing down his face and Reid could feel the taste of it in his mouth. It soon froze because of the intense cold. Reid revived sufficiently to give the thumbs-up' sign and carry on with the mission and they managed to accurately bomb the target and return to base.

Reid had memorised the course to the target and could therefore carry on with the mission without the compasses, Düsseldorf was still some 50 minutes away. After dropping the plane's bomb load, Reid flew back as best he could, navigating by the stars and the moon. The elevators trimming tabs had been shot away making control difficult, they had to always hold the stick with both hands, with the help of the engineer and the bomb aimer who was called on to help. The exertion started Reid's head bleeding again. They kept the Lancaster going and got through despite being caught in searchlights and heavy anti-aircraft fire over The Netherlands coast. At times Reid lapsed into semi-consciousness. (The flight engineer, Sergeant J Norris was later awarded the Conspicuous Gallantry Medal.)

Reid stated that: *'Then I saw a drome beneath us. I flashed the distress signal with the landing lamp. Just as we touched down the undercarriage collapsed. It had been shot through and we went on our tummy for about 50 yards. No one was hurt in the crash'.*

Convalescing in hospital, Reid recounted his experience: *'I just saw a blinding flash, and I lost about 2,000 feet before I could pull out again. I felt as if my head had been blown off – just the sort of feeling you get at the time. Other members of the crew shouted: 'Are you alright?' I felt alright. I resumed course and managed to get my goggles on. My shoulder was a bit stiff, and it felt as if someone had hit me with a hammer'.*

From the Operations Record Book of 61 Squadron, November 1943:

3/4th, Lancaster LM 360

F/L. W. Reid. Captain, Sgt J. W. Norris, Flt. Eng., F/S J. S. Jeffries. Nav., Sgt. L. G. Rolton. A.B., F/S. J. J. Mann. WT/AG., F/S. S. G. Baldwin. A.G.1., F/S. A.F. Emerson. A.G.2.

Up Time 16.59, Down Time 22.01

F/L Reid was attacked by enemy night fighters on the way out, but although he and Flight Engineer were wounded, and the Navigator killed outright he proceeded on to bomb the target. On returning a crash landing was made at RAF Shipman. (USAAF operated air base in Norfolk.)

Lena, Reid's mother, was busy feeding the children at Baillieston School when a reporter walked in and asked her for some details about her son. She asked: *Why, what's he done? I knew about my son's bomber being badly damaged on one trip, but I never guessed this would be the result'.* This was the first she had heard that he had won the VC: *'When I saw him in hospital after he was wounded, he did not want to tell me anything about the raid'.*

At that time, Helena Murdoch Reid, 97 Swinton Crescent, Baillieston, had lost her husband, William, and in July 1940 her eldest son, Sergeant George Reid, 28, air gunner with RAF 15 Squadron had been shot down over Belgium.

Reid was visited in hospital by Air Vice Marshal Cochrane, who asked him why he didn't turn back. Reid said that he thought it safer to go on rather than turning back among all the other planes all flying in the same direction. Cochrane then added: *'It's as if they all said, "That bugger, Jock, he went on even though he was badly wounded, so we can't turn back just because of a faulty altimeter, or something like that'.*

In July of the following year, 1944, Reid was shot down and captured whilst bombing a V-1 rocket site at Rilly-la-Montagnes, near Reims, France. He had been posted to the second flight of RAF 617 Squadron, the famous 'Dambusters'. They had just released a massive 'Tallboy' earthquake bomb at 12,000 feet when they were struck by bombs from an aircraft above them. The bomb ploughed through his aeroplane's fuselage, severing all the control cables, and weakening its structure. Reid gave the order to bail-out and later recalled his Lancaster going into a spin. He was pinned to his seat but managed to reach overhead and release the escape hatch panel. He then recalled being outside the aircraft with the wireless operator, the two of them being the only survivors. Bill landed heavily by parachute, breaking one of his arms in the fall. Within an hour they were made prisoners of war, eventually ending up in Stalag Luft III at Luckenwalde, southwest of Berlin. He was released after ten months by Soviet troops, whilst they were on a forced march to a new pow camp.

From the Operations Record Book of RAF 617 Squadron:

Woodhall Spa. 31 July 1944

16 Lancaster's and 2 Mosquito aircraft were detailed for operations. All aircraft took off successfully, the target being a railway tunnel at Rilly-la-Montagne. The operation was successful, several bombs being seen to burst close to the aiming point. "S" (P/L. Reid) bale out, but it could not be confirmed that they were members of his crew, which consisted of F/L. Reid V.C. (124438) (Pilot), 909536 F/Sgt. Stewart D.G.W. (F/Eng), F/O. J.O. Peltier (J.17546) (Nav), P/O L.G. Rolton (171066) (A/B.), F/O D. Luker (134635?) (W/Op), Holt A.A. (M.U.) and 1378696 W/O. Hutton J.W. (R.G.). The weather at base was cloudy with poor visibility at first, becoming moderate. Fair early, in evening, becoming cloudy.

Operations Summary.

During the month 107 operational sorties were despatched, comprising 234 hrs. 45 mins operational day flying and 129 hrs. 35 mins night operational flying. Of these, 1 aircraft was lost and 29 failed to complete missions. A total of 256 hrs. 25 mins flying day was carried out on training. A total of 431.5 tons of bombs was dropped operationally

Holt A A was Flight Sergeant Albert Arthur Holt (1159886). F/O D. Luker is not listed as being killed and may have survived. The crew who died are buried at Clichy Northern Cemetery, just north of the city of Paris, 150 km to the west.

In a postcard to his mother in Baillieston, Reid wrote: *'Again I tell you not to worry about me, mother, and you had better have another holiday. It will do no good moping about me'.*

After the war, Reid was an agricultural degree student at Glasgow University, in Hertfordshire; he was the national cattle and sheep adviser to the Spillers company; later director of MacRobert Farms (Douneside) Ltd., and eventually manager of Douneside Group Farms, Tarland. In 1987, he was one of the successful applicants for the Freedom of the City of London. Reid was president of the British Legion in Crieff and honorary life president of the Air Crew Association. Coatbridge Secondary School affectionately referred to Wiliam Reid as 'Weelum or Whelam'. A second brother of Reid was killed during the war.

Reid and his wife Violet retired to Crieff for the last 20 years of his life. He passed away on 28 November 2001 aged 79 and is buried in the Ford Road Cemetery, Crieff. The couple had a son Graeme and a daughter Susan. Violet died on 25 September 2019.

Bill Reid always claimed that he had done no more than his duty. He was well known as a modest, kindly, family man. His wife Violet Gallagher was unaware that he was a VC holder until they were married in 1952, she was, he confessed, "a wee bit impressed".

With precision timing, four Tornado aircraft of Reid's famous 617 Squadron based at RAF Lossiemouth approached at low level at 1.30 pm over Crieff, overflying the church in diamond formation. Precisely as they passed over the church, the rearmost aircraft peeled off into a vertical climb and powered upwards into the clouds, the 'Missing Man' formation.

Medal entitlement of Flight Lieutenant William Reid, 61 Squadron, Royal Air Force Volunteer Reserve:

Victoria Cross

1939-45 Star

Air Crew Europe Star – clasp: 'France & Germany'

War Medal (1939-45)

Queen Elizabeth II Coronation Medal (1953)

Queen Elizabeth II Silver Jubilee Medal (1977)

Act Flt Lt William REID RAFVR

"The KING has been graciously pleased to confer the VICTORIA CROSS on the undermentioned officer in recognition of most conspicuous bravery: —

Acting Flight Lieutenant William REID (124438), Royal Air Force Volunteer Reserve, No. 61 Squadron.

On the night of November 3rd, 1943, Flight Lieutenant Reid was Pilot, and Captain of a Lancaster aircraft detailed to attack Dusseldorf.

Shortly after crossing the Dutch coast, the pilot's windscreen was shattered by fire from a Messerschmitt no. Owing to a failure in the heating circuit, the rear gunner's hands were too cold for him to open fire immediately or to operate his microphone and so give warning of danger; but after a brief delay he managed to return the Messerschmitt's fire and it was driven off.

During the fight with the Messerschmitt, Flight Lieutenant Reid was wounded in the head, shoulders and hands. The elevator trimming tabs of the aircraft were damaged and it became difficult to control. The rear turret, too, was badly damaged and the communications system and compasses were put out of action. Flight Lieutenant Reid ascertained that his crew were unscathed and, saying nothing about his own injuries, he continued his mission.

Soon afterwards, the Lancaster was attacked by a Focke Wulf 190. This time, the enemy's fire raked the bomber from stem to stern. The rear gunner replied with his only serviceable gun, but the state of his turret made accurate aiming impossible. The navigator was killed, and the wireless operator fatally injured. The mid-upper turret was hit, and the oxygen system put out of action. Flight Lieutenant Reid was again wounded and the flight engineer, though hit in the forearm, supplied him with oxygen from a portable supply.

Flight Lieutenant Reid refused to be turned from his objective and Dusseldorf was reached some 50 minutes later. He had memorised his course to the target and had continued in such a normal manner that the bomb-aimer, who was cut off by the failure of the communications system, knew nothing of his captain's injuries or of the casualties to his comrades. Photographs show that, when the bombs were released, the aircraft was right over the centre of the target.

Steering by the pole star and the moon, Flight Lieutenant Reid then set course for home. He was growing weak from loss of blood. The emergency oxygen supply had given out. With the windscreen shattered, the cold was intense. He lapsed into semi-consciousness. The flight engineer, with some help from the bomb-aimer, kept the Lancaster in the air despite heavy anti-aircraft fire over the Dutch coast.

The North Sea crossing was accomplished. An airfield was sighted. The captain revived, resumed control and made ready to land. Ground mist partially obscured the runway lights. The captain was also much bothered by blood from his head wound getting into his eyes. But he made a safe landing although one leg of the damaged undercarriage collapsed when the load came on.

Wounded in two attacks, without oxygen, suffering severely from cold, his navigator dead, his wireless operator fatally wounded, his aircraft crippled and defenceless, Flight Lieutenant Reid showed superb courage and leadership in penetrating a further 200 miles into enemy territory to attack one of the most strongly defended targets in Germany, every additional mile increasing the hazards of the long and perilous journey home. His tenacity and devotion to duty were beyond praise.

Notes:

Battle of Britain pilot, Squadron Leader Hardie McHardie, an artist from Arran and a friend of Reid was also in Stalag Luft III with him. McHardie helped dig that camp's famous escape tunnels and was due to be in the second batch of escapees. This attempt was abandoned after 50 in the first batch were murdered by the Gestapo. McHardie returned to Arran, bought a ship's lifeboat and spent his spare time gathering and marketing shellfish.

RAF 617 Squadron at the time of Reid's VC was led by Wing Commander Leonard Cheshire, who would later also win the VC to add to his DSO and DFC. Reid was invested with his VC by King George VI at Buckingham Palace on 11 June 1944

Bill's VC was sold at auction in London in November 2009 for £348.000.

VICTORIA CROSS WINNERS: 1939-1945. (CHP 794) Portrait of William Reid RAF, awarded the Victoria Cross: Germany, 3 November 1940. Copyright: © IWM. Original Source: http://www.iwm.org.uk/collections/item/object/205069953

Celebrating Success of Douneside Herd

At last night's complimentary dinner to Lady MacRobert and Mr William Heughan, directors of MacRobert Farms, Ltd. (Douneside), l. to r.—Mrs V. Fradley, Flt./Lt. William Reid, V.C.; Lady MacRobert, and Mr Peter N. M'Farlane.

Aberdeen Press and Journal 3 August 1950

FLIGHT LIEUT. WILLIAM REID, V.C.
The Victoria Cross has been awarded to a Lancaster bomber pilot, Flight Lieut. Reid, who had an amazing series of adventures during a recent heavy raid on Dusseldorf. With the front of the cockpit shot away, and himself and his crew all injured, Reid bombed the target, and returned to England.

DAILY LIFE IN STALAG LUFT III IN SAGAN, MARCH 1942-JANUARY 1945 (HU 21030) A panoramic view of Stalag Luft III, Sagan. In the middle foreground there is a group of POWs playing volleyball with a line of laundry behind them. Around entrances to the hut's POWs can be seen doing their daily tasks and resting. Copyright: © IWM. Original Source: http://www.iwm.org.uk/collections/item/object/205184726

3 Margaret Watson-Watt

'The Mother of Radar', Margaret Robertson was born in St Catherine's Road, Perth. Her father, David, was a draughtsman and her mother was employed in Campbell's Dyeworks. Her father was a partner for a few years, along with Alexander Robertson in the Perth Foundry business, Paul Street, off the Old High Street. Margaret was educated at Perth Academy where she showed an aptitude for languages. She worked for a brief time in the office at Perth Foundry. In 1904, she left Perth to go to London where her father had taken up a position of draughtsman. Her grandfather, Mr D Robertson was the founder of the stationers and booksellers' business at 95-97 High Street, Perth.

Shortly after being married, Margaret returned to Perth for a visit – in 1916 – along with her husband Robert Alexander Watson Watt. Watt was born in Brechin, 13 April 1892, and is regarded as the 'Inventor of Radar'. At the very least, he was a significant contributor to its development. Watson was not the only person to have thought about the possibilities in this area, but he was the first to produce a workable solution. Watson Watt added a hyphen between his last names to become 'Watson-Watt' in the 1940s. In his autobiography 'Three Steps to Victory' he introduced the unsubstantiated fact that he was a descendant of James Watt of Greenock, the inventor of the first practical steam engine in 1776.

Watson-Watt attended University College in Dundee, where he was introduced to wireless telegraphy, radio frequency oscillators and wave propagation while assisting Professor William Peddie, the Chair of Physics at Dundee. At the age of eighteen, Robert won a prize in Chemistry and graduated with a BSc in Engineering in 1912.

Margaret was a teacher in Dundee and had studied at University College. She attended evening classes where her future husband was the lecturer. She also went to evening classes in metalwork and learned to make jewellery. Watson-Watt and Margaret Robertson married on 20 July 1916 in Hammersmith, London. That year he joined the Meteorological Office which was interested in his ideas for using radio to detect thunderstorms.

They started their married life living in a wooden hut between Aldershot and Farnborough, the Wireless Station of Air Ministry Meteorological Office. A second hut was used for their joint research work. Margaret used her jewellery-making skills to repair Robert's devices, soldering connections and making repairs to the apparatus. At the time, Watson-Watt described his radio apparatus as little more than lengths of wire. Margaret's other duty was that of recorder and observer of the radio experiments. Every two or three days, she would cycle into Aldershot to buy supplies for the home.

During the Great War, Margaret had another useful skill, she transcribed messages from Paris in Morse-

Code and passed them on the British High Command in Aldershot. She also listened to the time signals from Berlin and Paris, with a stopwatch in one hand and a telephone in the other, and at precisely the correct moment gave the word 'Go' to the command HQ. They then sounded three 'pips' on a siren. This was the forerunner of the BBC Time Signal.

In 1923, Watson-Watt set sail for the Indian Ocean and the Red Sea for three months to study atmospherics. Margaret later joined him in Alexandria, and they set up tents on the outskirts of Cairo full of equipment for further experiments. Armed Bedouins carried off the tent with the apparatus.

Without the apparatus, they moved further up the Nile to the Helouan (Helwan) Observatory. The government of Sudan then invited them to Khartoum and provided them with a house. Here they conducted more experiments into atmospherics with some of the best thunderstorms they had ever seen.

Back in Britain, Margaret became a homemaker again until nine years later when she once again became the assistant to Watson-Watt in his research work. This time they were off to Tromsø, Norway, two hundred miles within the Arctic Circle.

Watson-Watt joined the Meteorological Office, which in 1927 was amalgamated with the National Physical Laboratory (NPL) – with Watson-Watt at the head. In 1933, he became Superintendent of the NPL in Teddington. By 1934, he was the head of Radio Research at Ditton Park near Slough. He was approached by the Air Ministry who asked him whether a radio wave could be used to produce a death-ray. The Germans had claimed that they had invented a device that could do this. Working with Arnold Wilkins at the time he assured the Air Ministry that this was, of course, impossible, but it did give him the chance to put forward the idea of using radio to detect aircraft. Soon Watson-Watt and Wilkins demonstrated to the Air Ministry official and physicist, A P Rowe (also known as Jimmy Rowe).

On 2 April 1935, Watson-Watt was granted a patent for radar and by June was detecting aircraft up to fifteen miles away. By the end of the year, this had risen to up to sixty miles. What Watson-Watt eventually produced was the highly effective Chain Home radar system. This proved to invaluable during the air battles that were to come.

Initially, the work of the Telecommunications Research Establishment (TRE) was carried out was at Bawdsey near Felixstowe. This was felt to be a bit unsafe as it was just a short German E-boat run over the English Channel should war break out. The name of the unit changed in 1936 to the Air Ministry Experimental Station (AMES). When the war broke, out the team rushed to Dundee University where the Rector was only dimly aware of an earlier conversation with Watson-Watt about them working there.

Part of the team, now at Dundee, which was working on Airborne Interception Radar (AI), was sent along to RAF Perth (Scone) airfield to work. This was not entirely suitable and later in the year, the main part of the team was moved down to RAF St Athan in the Vale of Glamorgan, Wales. This also was found to be unsuitable, and the team was moved again to Worth Matravers in Dorset near Swanage. By May 1940, the distance between the teams proved unworkable and the AMES team left Dundee to a new location near the AI team at Worth Matravers.

Watson-Watt managed to cut through red-tape and have the Radar stations staffed by Women's Auxiliary Air Force (WAAF) members who did the calculations and passed on the enemy raid information by telephone to Fighter Command. The first five coastal radar-manned stations were up and running by July 1938, By the time the Second World War started on 1 September 1939, there were nineteen operational radar stations.

Watson-Watt filed patents in 1935 and 1936 on a system to identify friend or foe (IFF) aircraft. The first active IFF transponder was first used experimentally in 1939. Watson-Watt had an assistant, Edward Bowen, who came up with an airborne radar system to help pilots detect enemy planes beyond visibility. Watson-Watt also helped develop the use of radar for use by the Royal Navy against German U-boats.

In 1942, Watson-Watt was knighted becoming Sir Robert Alexander Watson-Watt, KCB, FRS, FRAeS. In 1952, Watson-Watt was given £50,000 by the British Government for his work on radar. Margaret filed a divorce petition against Robert on grounds of adultery, and they divorced that year. Margaret returned to Perth, purchasing Dunalistair, Muirton Bank, Perth. Watson-Watt moved to Canada where he set up an engineering consultancy. In Canada, he married his second wife, Jean Wilkinson. Whilst in Canada, he ironically received a speeding ticket from a policeman using, a radar gun. Robert wrote an ironic poem ('Rough Justice') afterwards:

Pity Sir Robert Watson-Watt,

strange target of this radar plot

And thus, with others I can mention,

the victim of his own invention.

His magical all-seeing eye

enabled cloud-bound planes to fly

but now by some ironic twist

it spots the speeding motorist

and bites, no doubt with legal wit,

the hand that once created it.

Jean Wilkinson died in 1964 and Watson-Watt returned to Scotland and in 1966 at the age of seventy-four, he married for the third time, to Dame Katherine Jane Trefusis Forbes who was sixty-seven at the time.

Watson-Watt lived in the winter in London with Dame Katherine Forbes and in the summer at 'The Observatory', the home of Dame Katherine in Pitlochry. Dame Katherine was the first director of the Women's Auxiliary Air Force (1939-1943). She died in 1971.

Watson-Watt died two years later – in 1973 – in Inverness, age 81, and is buried along with Forbes in the churchyard of the Episcopal Church in Pitlochry.

Margaret, Lady Watson-Watt, passed an Italian 'A' level course in 1972, only one of six to pass the exam and while in her eighties. She celebrated her 102nd birthday on 3 May 1988 with a sherry party and specially made cake at St Johnstoun Nursing Home, Perth. She passed away peacefully on Wednesday 7 September 1988 at St Johnstoun Nursing Home. A funeral service was held in St Stephen's Parish Church, Muirton and she was interred thereafter in Dunning Cemetery.

Watson Watt once paid tribute to the value of Margaret Robertson Watson-Watt's contribution:

'The technique we worked out in those years has been extended over the whole field of radio research, and in that sense was the forerunner of the experiments that led to radio location'.

The couple had no children.

Notes:

Campbell's Dyeworks was in St Catherine's Road. It was destroyed by fire 20 May 1919 and then amalgamated with Messrs J Pullar & Sons, Limited. John Pullar who established Pullar's was apprenticed to Peter Campbell in 1814/16.

Perth Foundry was in Paul Street. An iron steamship, the 'Eagle' was built by Perth Foundry in 1836.

RESEARCH NOTE from Steve Nicoll 23 November 2021

Robert Watson-Watt 'was born Robert Alexander Watson Watt, no hyphen. Watson and Watt are however family surnames. The hyphen appears later in his life when he introduced it into his signature and literature. His birth certificate is clear, no hyphen and registered as Robert Alexander Watson Watt'. In addition, 'the connection with James Watt is unproven by BDM records on both individuals which separate them by timelines, geography and social status. Sadly, it's a genealogy connection that continues to be repeated on numerous websites and publications. There is no established connection between two of Scotland's greatest engineers.'

Margaret and Robert Watson-Watt, Perthshire Advertiser 21 June 1941

Margaret and Robert Watson-Watt

Perth Foundry Paul Street 1968

SIR ROBERT ALEXANDER WATSON-WATT, CB.,LL.B.,FRS. (CH 13863) Original wartime caption: Caption as for CH.13862. Copyright: © IWM. Original Source: http://www.iwm.org.uk/collections/item/object/205453237

4 Steward Robert Russell Martin

Robert Russell Martin was an incredibly brave seaman who served in World War Two with the Royal Navy. Robert Russell Martin, C/LX 22660 was a Royal Navy steward who served aboard two ships, *HMS Mohawk* and *HMS Welshman*. He experienced on very many occasions being bombed by aircraft and attacked by U-boats, the list of sea actions that he was involved in is staggering. From day one he was involved in the Battle of the River Forth, then Dunkirk and no less than six of the major convoys sent to relieve the island of Malta.

Martin was married with two children and assisted his mother in her fruit business at 39 South Methven Street, Perth. He was the eldest son of Agnes R Martin of 290 High Street, Perth, and the husband of Margaret Young Martin. Martin's Fruit Bazaar has now been in business in Perth for 102 years, starting in the Old High Street with a horse and cart and moving to South Methven Street in 1931.

Robert was on the **HMS Mohawk**, a Tribal-class destroyer when it was bombed by one of twelve Luftwaffe Junkers JU 88 aircraft in the Firth of Forth October on 16 October 1939. When bombs straddled the ship, landing 15 yards off the ship's starboard side, the upward blast of the explosions scattered splinters and caused extensive casualties on the bridge and upper decks. The captain was wounded, 15 of the ship's company including the 1st Lieutenant were killed, and 30 were injured from the ships compliment of 190. This was the first 'real' German air raid over the United Kingdom during World War II, the **Battle of the River Forth**.

The Germans had spotted a large British capital ship, *HMS Hood* during aerial reconnaissance earlier that morning, and that was their primary target. Initially no air raid warning was sounded, but then sirens did go off in some places. In Perth, which was not threatened at all, residents were kept in shelters for several hours. The nine German *Kampfgeschwader 30* raiders under the command of Hauptmann Helmet Pohle were intercepted by RAF No. 603 Squadron (City of Edinburgh) and No. 602 (City of Glasgow) Squadron. Flight Lieutenant Pat Gifford from 603 Squadron shot down the first German aircraft that day. RAF 603 Squadron were based at RAF Turnhouse, now Edinburgh Airport and RAF 602 were at Drem, not far away our National Museum of Flight at East Fortune.

The Captain of *HMS Mohawk*, Commander Richard Frank Jolly subsequently died of his wounds. Jolly was wounded in the stomach but refused to leave his post or to receive medical attention. He continued to direct the *Mohawk* for the 35-mile passage to the dock, which took 80 minutes. After bringing the ship into port, he collapsed and died five hours later. Jolly was considered for the Victoria Cross; he was eventually awarded posthumously the Empire Gallantry medal (later the George Cross).

The Captain of his Flotilla reported, *"Commander Jolly was an imperturbable Commander of careful judgment who devoted his energies to perfecting his ship and ship's company for battle. His fearlessness and honesty in counsel were remarkable, and he proved his bravery and devotion to his wounded men when for a long period he manoeuvred his ship despite a mortal wound".*

In May 1940, *HMS Mohawk* was actively working off the coast of The Netherlands and Robert was on board when the ship made a score of trips to **Dunkirk** during the evacuation of Allied soldiers from 26 May 1940 to 4 June 1940. *HMS Mohawk* was active in the Mediterranean Sea, bombarding Bardia in eastern Libya on 3 January 1941 and the following week was part of the escort force for the of **Operation Excess** convoy bringing supplies to Malta. When *HMS Gallant* stuck a mine, which blew off her bow, *Mohawk* was detached and detailed to tow her stern-first to Malta. After refuelling she went to the assistance of the light cruisers *HMS Southampton* and *HMS Gloucester* which had been attacked by JU 88's. *Southampton*'s fires were burning out of control, and she had to be scuttled.

During the **Battle of Cape Matapan** (27-29 March 1941) *HMS Mohawk* was escorting battleships of the Mediterranean Fleet when the 14th Destroyer Flotilla (*HMS Jervis, Janus, Mohawk, and Nubian*, commanded by Philip Mack) was detached at dusk on 28th March 1941 to try and find and sink the severely damaged Italian Regia Marina Battleship *Vittorio Vento*. They spotted the burning Italian heavy cruiser *Zara* on the morning of the 29th. She had been crippled by British Battleships the previous evening, they picked up survivors and torpedoed the wreck. One hour later they rescued the crew of the Italian heavy cruiser *Pola* which had been hit by a torpedo earlier in the day. They then sank the *Pola* with three of their own torpedoes. The Battle of Cape Matapan was described by the naval historian Vincent O'Hara as "Italy's greatest defeat at sea, subtracting from its order of battle a cruiser division, but the battle was hardly decisive."

From 1-6 April, HMS Mohawk as part of the 14th DF escorted a convoy from Egypt to Greece and although the Luftwaffe attacked them, they were not damaged. They arrived in Malta on the night of 10/11 April 1941 and were given orders to attack Italian supply convoys to Libya. On their third patrol they attacked a small convoy of five cargo ships and three destroyers in the early hours of 16 April 1941.

HMS Mohawk and *HMS Nubian* were in the rear of the flotilla formation, the lead ships opening fire at 02.20 am. Mohawk withheld fire as all targets were being engaged and when the leading Italian destroyer *Luca Tarigo* turned back, all ships opened fire. Whilst the Italian ship was sinking, it managed to fire two torpedoes. The first of these struck *HMS Mohawk* as she was turning to avoid being rammed by the German freighter *SS Arta* shortly after 2.45 am. The torpedo hit on the starboard side knocking out both aft gun mounts and blowing off the upper stern. The Chief Engineer reported that *Mohawk* could still move but another torpedo stuck at 02.53 am causing the aft boiler to explode and the upper deck to split down the middle. *HMS Mohawk* capsized one minute later with the loss of forty-one crewmen. *HMS Janus* put 4 shells into *Mohawk's* buoyant forecastle to allow her to sink underwater in the shallow waters off the Kerkennah Islands, position 34.56N 11.42E - 41 of the ship's company lost their lives and 168 survivors were rescued.

HMS Welshman was an Abdiel-class fast cruiser minelayer, laid down on 8 June 1939 and commissioned in late August 1941. She was built at the R & W Hawthorn Leslie & Co shipyard at Hebburn-on-Tyne and launched on 4 September 1940. *HMS Welshman* first saw service with the Home Fleet at Scapa Flow and later, on 23 September 1941 was attached to the 1st Minelaying Squadron at Kyle of Lochalsh. Her first operation was to lay mines in the Butt of Lewis which was part of the Northern Barrage.

In November 1941, there was a cancelled plan to lay mines off the Norwegian coast and in December she was detached to the English Channel for minelaying operations. On 15 December 1941, *HMS Welshman* departed to lay mines in the Bay of Biscay. The German battleships, *Scharnhorst* and *Gneisenau* were docked at Brest, and this was an attempt to prevent them from returning to commerce raiding in the Atlantic.

On 6 January 1941, *HMS Welshman* sailed for Gibraltar, Freetown, and Takoradi, transporting stores and personnel. On 1 February 1942, *HMS Welshman* was back at Plymouth; on 3 February 1942, she was deployed to Dover for minelaying operations in the English Channel. On 4, 5, 7, 9 February, she laid mines between Normandy and Boulogne, the route that the German Kriegsmarine Battleships, *Scharnhorst* and *Gneisenau* might take if they chose to return to Germany (The 'Channel Dash' of 11-13 February 1942).

On 12, 13, 15, and 18 February 1942, they were back laying mines in the Bay of Biscay. During March, *HMS Welshman* had a refit in a Tyneside shipyard. April 14, 17, & 20 saw more mine laying in the Bay of Biscay. On 21 April, she was transferred to Port ZA (Kyle of Lochalsh) but was diverted to Plymouth for conversion to carry petrol and other stores.

On competition of the conversion work, she set sail to join Force H, in Gibraltar to help support Malta, which was under siege by Axis forces. The Luftwaffe and Reggia Aeronautica air forces were relentlessly attacking the island and its supply convoys. In the early months of 1942, supplies of food, medicines, ammunition, spare parts, and fuel were almost running out and were desperately required. On 8 May 1942, *HMS Welshman* sailed from Gibraltar to Malta with 240 tons of stores and RAF ground crew to be transferred to the island. Apart from food and stores, the ship carried 100 spare Rolls-Royce Merlin engines.

This was part of **Operation Bowery**, an Anglo-American operation to deliver Supermarine Spitfires ('Club Runs'), desperately needed to bolster the island's defences. The convoy included the aircraft carriers *USS Wasp* and *HMS Eagle*. On 9 May 1942, 64 Spitfires took off and 61 arrived on the island. *HMS Welshman* was disguised as a (Free) French destroyer, the *FFS Léopard*. The real *Léopard* was currently in a Kingston-Upon-Hull dock being converted to an escort destroyer.

HMS Welshman was spotted twice by German aircraft but maintained a non-aggressive appearance and passed without harm – as a non-belligerent. On entering the Grand Harbour at Malta *HMS Welshman* detonated two mines with her paravanes (towed underwater 'glider') and sustained some damage. She discharged her cargo and returned to Gibraltar.

HMS Welshman arrived back at Gibraltar on 12 May 1942 and on 16 May 1942, set sail to Yarrow Shipbuilders yard at Scotstoun, Glasgow, for repairs. On 29 June 1942, she returned to Gibraltar arriving 1 June 1942. On entry to the harbour, she sustained damage to her bow and propeller shaft in collision with a tug. She was repaired in Gibraltar and set sail on 11 June 1942 for Malta as part of **Operation Harpoon**. The next day she was dispatched from the convoy and made her way independently to Malta arriving 15 June 1942. After she had offloaded her supplies, she returned to reinforce the convoy which was under heavy air attacks. On 16 June 1942, she returned to Malta with the two remaining merchant ships and their escort.

After returning to Gibraltar, she sailed to Scotstoun for repair and a boiler clean, *HMS Welshman* took part in three more convoy operations to Malta. **Operation Pinpoint** left Gibraltar on 14 July 1942. On 15 July, *HMS Welshman* made an independent run close to the coast of Algeria to try and divert attention from the convoy. She was shadowed by Axis aircraft and attacked by fighters, bombers, and torpedo bombers.

Operation Pedestal – with supplies dwindling in Malta – this was the largest convoy to date set sail from Great Britain (3 August 1942), passing through the Strait of Gibraltar on the night of 9 August 1942. It consisted of 14 merchant ships, including the large oil tanker, *SS Ohio*, and 44 escort warships, including the aircraft carriers, *HMS Eagle*, *HMS Indomitable* and *HMS Victorious.* The convoy was heavily attacked, the *Ohio* arrived undertow. The cruisers, *HMS Eagle*, *HMS Cairo*, *HMS Manchester*, and the destroyer *HMS Foresight* were sunk and there was serious damage to the other warships. Of the merchant ships, only three arrived, two on the 13th and one more on the 14th. *Ohio* eventually arrived lashed to two destroyers and towed by a third. She later broke in two in Valetta Harbour, not before most of the fuel had been unloaded. *HMS Welshman* arrived on 16 August 1942.

The last big Malta convoy operation for *HMS Welshman* was **Operation Train** on 28 October 1942. Despite attempts by German U-boats, Italian ships, and aircraft to intercept this convoy, none were successful. Ten Italian submarines were patrolling, and one Junkers JU88 aircraft managed to drop a single bomb – it just missed the aircraft carrier *HMS Furious*. Furious flew off 29 Spitfires for Malta's defence.

On 11 November 1942, *HMS Welshman* sailed to Algiers with supplies for the support of **Operation Torch**, the Anglo-American invasion of French Morocco and Algeria. After that, she collected torpedoes from Haifa in Palestine and even carried seed potatoes to Malta. Mines were laid in the Skerki Channel (Strait of Sicily), and she transported troops from Beirut, Lebanon to Cyprus. By 30 January 1943, *HMS Welshman* was back laying mines in the Skerki Channel, and the next day she went back to Alexandria to load stores and personnel for Tobruk. At 17.45 hours on 1 February 1943, to the east of Tobruk, the German U-boat, U-617 fired a spread of four torpedoes at *HMS Welshman*. Two hit the cruiser, one caused a boiler explosion and serious flooding of the mine deck caused instability which could not be corrected.

After two hours, the ship capsized and sank quickly by the stern. Onboard *HMS Welshman* were 289 officers and men, 165 were killed and 124 survived. Of the passengers, two were civilians and four were aircrew who had been severely burned in an aircraft crash on Malta. The ship's captain William Howard Dennis Friedberger, DSO, RN, along with five officers and 112 others were rescued by *HMS Tetcott* and *HMS Belvoir*. Another six people were rescued by small craft from Tobruk.

Steward Robert Russell Martin is commemorated at the Chatham Naval Memorial in Kent, England. Twenty-four-year-old Robert Russell Martin had been in the Royal Navy for five years.

Albrecht Brandi the captain of U-617 identified the *Welshman* as a Dido class cruiser. He fired a spread of four torpedoes and observed two hits followed by an explosion which he assessed was the ships boiler exploding.

Extract from the War Diary of U-617, patrol of 27 January-13 February 1943:

16.05 Hydrophone effect at 355°

17.35 An unescorted cruiser at bearing 350° true. Inclination 5°, bows left, range 3,000m. I manoeuvre into an attacking position. Her shadow is very faint in the periscope.

17.45 Wind NW 3, sea 2, 6/10 overcast. Visibility 2,000m. Almost completely dark. Spread of four torpedoes fired. After 88 sec, two heavy detonations followed by a third. probably her boilers going up.

17.55 Surfaced. Cruiser capsized, sinking stern first. Several searchlights on land at a bearing of 180° true. We withdraw, course 0°.

18.13 Radar-warning readings of a number of ships on the 140-cm wave, volume 5. Alarm dive.

18.25 Surfaced. several more radar readings. A land-based station that sweeps in our direction every so often.

20.00 Wind NW 3, sea 2, rain, visibility 500m. I haul off to the north to reload and transmit W/T report.

2112 Outgoing W/T transmission. "At 17.45 in position Qu. (CO) 6776 hit cruiser with two torpedoes, depth 4 m, capsized and left sinking. 'Dido' type probably, but in darkness not sure. Brandi."

23.05 Dived to reload.

Brandi, Kptlt and Kmdt.

Notes:

The crucial **Operation Pedestal** convoy, especially the arrival of the oil tanker, SS Ohio was regarded as divine intervention by the people of Malta. August 15 is the Feast of the Assumption of Mary, and the Maltese regarded the arrival of Ohio into Grand Harbour as the answer to their prayers. The SS Ohio was an oil tanker built for the Texas Oil Company (now Texaco).

It had been agreed at the time in Malta, that if supplies were not received, they would surrender. **Operation Pedestal** delivered enough for Malta to last until mid-November. Over 500 merchant and Royal Navy sailors were killed getting the supplies to Malta. The siege of Malta was lifted by the advance of Allied forces towards Libya after the Second Battle of El Alamein (23 October 1942-11 November 1942) and **Operation Torch** (8-16 November 1942).

Success in stopping the supplies to Malta for the Axis forces would have made possible a combined German-Italian amphibious landing (Operation Herkules) of Malta, supported by German paratroopers (Fallschirmjäger).

Hauptmann Helmuth Pohle who led the first German aerial attack on the United Kingdom, the Battle of the River Forth was shot down and captured. He was the first German prisoner of war in World War II.

The movie, Malta Story made in 1953 depicts the heroic struggle to save the island. A Photographic Reconnaissance Unit (PRU) pilot, played by Alec Guinness arrives on the island and helps defend it. Scenes include photographing Axis invasion preparations, *HMS Welshman*, and the *SS Ohio* arriving lashed to the destroyers.

HMS MOHAWK (FL 16338) Stationary. Copyright: © IWM. Original Source:
http://www.iwm.org.uk/collections/item/object/205121262

THE WELSHMAN AT MALTA. 4 DECEMBER 1942, GRAND HARBOUR, VALLETTA, MALTA. (A 13681) HMS WELSHMAN, minelayer, leaving Grand Harbour. Copyright: © IWM. Original Source: http://www.iwm.org.uk/collections/item/object/205146958

HMS WELSHMAN LEAVING VALLETTA HARBOUR, MALTA. 18 JUNE 1942. (A 11127) HMS WELSHMAN with HMS GALLANT in the foreground. Copyright: © IWM. Original Source: http://www.iwm.org.uk/collections/item/object/205144770

HMS WELSHMAN AT MALTA. 16 JUNE 1942. (A 10839) Officers watching the unloading operation.
Copyright: © IWM. Original Source: http://www.iwm.org.uk/collections/item/object/205144509

General Charles De Gaulle inspecting sailors aboard Léopard, 24 June 1942

5 Flight Lieutenant William Fraser

William (Bill) Simpson Fraser (sometimes spelt Frazer) was born on 5 June 1908 to the Alexander family of 12 Pitcullen Crescent, Perth. The family business was Messrs Frazer & Sons, Clothiers (merchant tailors and complete outfitters) which was located at 55-59 High Street, Perth, with branches in Pitlochry, Kingussie and Aberfeldy. Alexander Frazer, his father, was the Lord Dean of Guild in Perth.

William Fraser attended Strathallan School, worked in a bank as a clerk in Perth and was well known as a moving spirit in local dramatic circles. In 1930, he received a theatrical appointment in London. The first few months were spent in Calcutta, India. He did not have a great start to his career and was often penniless, sleeping rough on the Embankment in London. Just before the Second World War, Fraser was running the Connaught Theatre in Worthing. He was there for seven years and in that time had acted in approximately 300 plays.

During the war, he was called up and served with the RAF in a RAF Special Liaison Unit reaching the rank of flight lieutenant. During this time, he met Eric Sykes and after the war, he met him again and gave him his first work as a writer for radio comedy. They worked together many times over the following years. Fraser is also credited with giving Peter Cushing his first acting job.

In 1942, Fraser married Betty Bowden, grand-daughter of the late rear Admiral Edward Kellyin, St Martin-in-the-Fields, London.

Fraser first appeared on television is The Tony Hancock Show (1956). He later joined The Army Game which led to a sequel for which he is probably best known and remembered, **Bootsie and Snudge**. There were very many roles in which he appeared on stage and TV over the years, many of them comedic parts. He appeared in 50 movies from 1938 through to 1987. In 1986 he won the Laurence Olivier Award for Best Comedy Performance for his stage role in the play, When We Are Married. In 1981, he was the subject of Eamonn Andrews, This Is Your Life.

When he was not acting, Fraser ran a sweetshop and tobacconist in Ilford Lane, Ilford. He later married again; to Pamela Cundell in 1981. Fraser died at the age of 79 on 9 September 1987 in Bushey, Hertfordshire. Pamela Cundell played Mrs Fox in the long-running TV comedy series, Dad's Army.

Special Liaison Units were connected to the Government Code and Cypher School at Bletchley Park, they oversaw the distribution of ULTRA intelligence.

Perth Man Weds Leading Lady

Mr W. S. Frazer and Miss Rosemary Elizabeth Bowden, after their
wedding in St Martin's-in-the-Fields.   "Worthing Herald" Photo.

In St Martin's-in-the-Fields, London, took place the marriage of Mr W. ("Bill") Simson Frazer, son of ex-Dean of Guild Alexander Frazer, late principal of Frazers of Perth, Ltd., and Mrs Frazer, Normandene, Christchurch Road, Worthing, to Miss Rosemary Elizabeth ("Betty") Bowden, London.

"Bill" Frazer was a well-known personality in Perth amateur dramatics before going south to take up professional stage work. After appearing in the London show "New Faces," and for a time with Ambrose and his band, he joined up as an aircraftman in the R.A.F.

When he ran the Worthing Repertory Company with Mr C. W. Bell, Miss Bowden was leading lady at the Connaught Theatre, Worthing. She is now leading lady with the Birmingham Repertory Company.

Daughter of Mr and Mrs W. E. Bowden, Prince of Wales Mansions, London, the bride was given away by her father. She was becomingly attired in a hyacinth blue two-piece costume.

Her mother wore a pink and black dress with a long black coat and black hat. The bridegroom's mother had chosen navy georgette and matching hat.

The ceremony was conducted by the bride's cousin, the Rev. Guy Bowden, Chaplain, R.A.F. Mr Robert Page was best man.

Guests at the reception in The Adelphi Theatre included Major Eric Maschwitz and Dame Sybil Thorndike. About 150 gifts were received.

Perthshire Advertiser 22 August 1942

within TWENTY-ONE DAYS *after its occurrence*; of a MARRIAGE *within* THREE DAYS *after its celebration*; and of a DEATH *within* EIGHT DAYS *after its event*. If *these rules are not complied with* PENALTIES *are exigible*.

BIRTHS.

BEATON—June 1, at Murthly, the wife of James Beaton, Haugh of Meikleour, of a daughter.

FRAZER—June 5, at 12 Pitcullen Crescent, Perth, Mrs Alexander Fraser, of a son.

MARRIAGES.

DODS — ANDERSON — June 8, at the County Hotel, Edinburgh, by the Rev. Thomas R. Rutherford, M.A., Dunkeld Cathedral, John, son of the late William Dods, Lugton, Dalkeith, to Lily Douglas,

Perthshire Advertiser 10 December 1913

6 Group Captain Robert Halley DFC & 2 bars, AFC

It is not well known that a young 24-year-old Perth aviator played a key role in bringing a period of peace to Afghanistan by bombing the city of Kabul in 1919. His bombing of Kabul had a considerable psychological effect, impacting on the morale of the Afghan citizens, and contributed to the quick bringing about of an armistice, thus ending the Third Afghan War or the British-Afghan War of 1919.

On 8 August 1919, 102 years ago, the war weary British and King Amanullah for the Afghans, jointly signed the Treaty of Rawalpindi, the fighting ending on August 19. The British relinquished their control over Afghan foreign affairs and Afghanistan became an independent country. Afghans celebrated their Independence Day to this day on the 19 of August.

Afghanistan has been a strategically important location throughout history. It was a gateway to India from the west and benefited handsomely from trade along the Silk Roads to China. Afghanistan was described as the 'Central Asian roundabout' where routes converged from the Middle East, the Indus Valley, through the passes of the Hindu Kush, the Eurasian Steppe and from China via the Tarim Basin. Many conquerors have come and went through this land including Alexander the Great and the Mongols. Many costly wars have been fought for control of this country.

The story of Perth born, Robert 'Jock' Halley is one of a man who was incredibly courageous and heroically determined to successfully target and attack the enemy. Halley was awarded the Distinguished Flying Cross (DFC) on three occasions.

Group Captain Robert 'Jock' Halley was born in Perth in November 1895. He was the second son of Bailie and Mrs Robert Halley, 5 Barossa Place, Perth. He was educated at Perth Academy and was following out agricultural work at Ardoch of Gallery, near Montrose when on reaching military age, he enlisted. Halley was a prominent member of Perthshire Cricket Club, second eleven and was regarded as a very good slow bowler.

He joined a cyclist unit of the Royal Highlanders (HCB) in February 1915 at Montrose. In February 1917, he transferred to the Royal Naval Air Service (RNAS) at RNASTE Vendôme, France taking his officers commission as a Probationary Flight Officer. The airfield operated over 100 Caudron G.III tractor biplane trainers and some Maurice Farman S.7 Longhorn pusher biplanes.

On graduation, he was posted to Naval 'A' Squadron (later 16 Naval Squadron and 216 Squadron R.A.F.), flying twin–engine Handley Page 0/100 (H.P.11) bomber aircraft. His observer was usually the American millionaire, Bobbie Reece.

Halley undertook as verified by his Flying Log-Book, over 20 night-bombing, open cockpit, biplane aircraft missions in all weathers before the end of the war. These were very daring long-distance strikes against targets in Köln (Cologne), Frankfurt, Stuttgart, and Mannheim (6 times). Naval "A" Squadron had been hurriedly formed at Manston in 1917, the Germans had been bombing London and cities in the south-east and civilians were crying out for reprisals. They were initially equipped with Handley Page 0/100-night bombers and sent out to Ochey aerodrome in France in order to bomb the German Rhine towns.

The first aircraft crash of the squadron occurred when Flight Lieutenant (later Captain) Halley came down in the middle of a wood at Chancenay, near Saint-Dizier. The machine (3140) practically buried itself in the mud and slush, only the engines being saved. All the occupants were uninjured.

One bombing mission of Robert Halley shows how he won his first bar to his DFC. And gives an indication of the challenges faced during such sorties. This account is from Peter Chapman's article for the 1914-18 Journal, "Frankfurt – By Night and By Day":

'In late August 1918, 216 Squadron were based at Autreville, France and were equipped with Handley Page 0/100 and Handley Page 0/400 twin-engined heavy bombers. These aircraft normally carried a crew of three – pilot, observer/navigator and gunner – and with a bomb load of up to 1650lbs were able to reach targets as far afield as Cologne, Stuttgart or Frankfurt.

The weather outlook on 24 August 1918 was not good, with a strong south-east wind blowing across much of eastern France and a weather forecast of severe thunderstorms approaching later that evening. Despite this, orders were received at the squadron to mount a maximum effort that night, the main target being the railway station and sidings at Frankfurt am Main, with the Burbach works at Saarbrucken as an alternative target, should a raid on Frankfurt not be possible.

Shortly after dusk the squadron's six serviceable aircraft took off individually, with a time lapse of a few minutes separating each take off, each aircraft being given the go ahead by the aerodrome officer via signal lamp. Soon after they had all departed, however, it became apparent to many crews that they would be faced with an almost impossible task to reach Frankfurt in the prevailing weather, and gradually all but two aircraft returned to their aerodrome with their bombs. One of the remaining two chose to bomb Boulay aerodrome, an alternate target, before also returning to Autreville.

The sixth aircraft that night was Handley Page 0/100 No. 3138, crewed by Captain Robert Halley, D.F.C. (pilot), Lieutenant Robert H. Reece, D.F.C. (observer/navigator) and 2nd Lieutenant C. W. Treleaven, a relatively new pilot in the squadron, who went along as their gunner. An experienced pairing, Halley and Reece had already undertaken a number of long-distance bombing sorties to targets such as Mannheim and Stuttgart, and both had been decorated with the Distinguished Flying Cross for their exploits.

After taking off and gaining height over their aerodrome, they steered a course to D lighthouse, one of a number of automated signalling lights on the Allied side of the lines which continually flashed a predetermined Morse Code letter as a guide to the night bombers. By figuring their ground speed and drift en route, the two men calculated that they could reach Frankfurt and return safely, despite the wind, if they steered a direct course there and back. Even then, their margin for error was almost nil, as they calculated they would have no more than five minutes over Frankfurt itself if they were to regain their own lines safely afterwards, and then with only 10 minutes of fuel to spare.

Steering a 39-degree course from D lighthouse, at an average altitude of 6000 feet, they encountered no more than sporadic flak from each town as they flew north of Saarburg, Bitsche and Pirmasens, then south of Kaiserslautern before crossing the Vosges mountains. They then crossed the Rhine River valley north of Oppenheim and flew on to Mainz. Here they followed the Main River to Frankfurt, arriving at their target at midnight. They were greeted by a heavy anti-aircraft barrage and numerous searchlights, but switching off engines briefly, Halley quickly glided their aircraft down and Reece dropped their bomb load, comprised of a single 550lb and four 112lb bombs, as close as possible to the Hauptbahnhof, or main railway station.

All of their bombs missed the intended target, falling in a ragged line across the properties alongside the river front, near the Westhafen. One bomb that landed on the Westhafen itself caused considerable damage to material stored there. This was possibly the 550lb bomb. The rest of the bombs damaged private property. Overall damage was considerable, however, amounting to 100,000 marks.

Having dropped their bombs, Halley and Reece hastily steered the most direct course for their own lines, over 100 miles away against a strengthening headwind. To add to their problems, they were approaching a storm ahead, which they dared not climb above as they did not have the fuel to spare. They elected instead to fly right underneath it, and found themselves being tossed about by fierce winds while being illuminated by lightning flashes and soaked by driving rain for hours. They were also being caught periodically in searchlights and their aircraft received numerous shrapnel hits from the accurate anti-aircraft fire, although none of these were serious enough to bring them down.

They finally cleared the first storm as they passed over Kaiserslautern, only to fly straight into another storm on the other side of the town. This storm too was cleared briefly, sufficient for them to again check their course and make a course correction, before they flew into a third and even more violent storm than those before. Fortunately, this storm was over quicker than its two predecessors, as Halley was unable to do more than keep the aircraft flying while it lasted, with no chance to follow a compass course. They arrived south of the Marne-Rhine canal as dawn was breaking, and steered for the nearest aerodrome, but shortly after crossing into friendly territory their engines stopped through lack of fuel, and the exhausted crew were forced to make a safe landing in a field near Luneville, eight and a half hours after they had set out.

Having striven against almost impossible weather, this brave crew had succeeded in reaching Frankfurt and dropping their bombs there, causing some considerable damage, albeit in the wrong place. They had then returned to a safe landing on their own side of the lines.

Their chief enemy this night was not the Germans however, but the weather, which may well have caused a less experienced crew to fail in their mission. They did not encounter enemy fighters during the entire flight but had been subjected to accurate anti-aircraft fire from various towns en route, as they were forced to fly low in a storm and were being illuminated by lightning flashes as well as searchlights from the ground.'

After this mission, Halley was awarded Bar to his DFC for this effort and he was selected to be one of only four pilots for a top-secret mission to attack 'the right spot', to bomb the German capital of Berlin. This would involve for the first time, non-stop flying by bomber aircraft all the way from England and back again.

The following message was received by RAF 216 squadron at the termination of WW1 hostilities:

D.S.O.

To O.C. No. 216 Squadron

Sender's Number G.O.C./211.

AAA On the Armistice being singed I would like to congratulate you on having materially assisted in bringing about this desirable result by creating demoralisation in Germany AAA It was only by the determination of the Ground Personnel in keeping the machines in an efficient condition and of the Pilots and Observers in getting the distance that this result was brought about AAA I hope to be able to come and thank you personally shortly AAA I would like you all to remember however that although the Armistice has been signed we must keep our weapons ready for instant use in case the enemy shows any signs of negligence to carry out the conditions AAA

From General Trenchard, H.Q., I.F.

(AAA was standard telegram-ese for a full stop)

Next Stop Berlin

Asleep in bed one night following another long night bombing raid on Mannheim, he was awoken and told he had to leave for England the following morning. A destroyer was waiting for him at Dunkirk and a car would meet him at Dover to take him to London. Halley was to fly the new Super Handley V/1500', very large, four-engine biplane designed to carry a 3,000 lb bomb load and fly from airfields in East Anglia, the distance to Berlin and back. The V/1500 was the very first aircraft to feature a gun turret in the tail and its size was not surpassed until the Boeing Super Fortress arrived in WW2. The Handley Page V/1500 had a wingspan of 126 ft and four Rolls Royce Eagle engines, between them developing 1,400hp.

Before these Berlin raids could be carried out, the war ended, the Armistice was agreed with Germany and World War One ended.

Flying to India

A few weeks later, in December 1918, Halley with Major A C S McLaren as co-pilot (and Maltese Terrier, 'Tiny'), Flight Sergeant Smith, Sergeant Crockett, and Sergeant Brown as the crew set off to fly to India from Ipswich in Handley Page V/1500 J1936, '*HMA Old Carthusian* '. They also carried a passenger, Brigadier General Norman D K McEwen who was to take over as AOC (Air Officer Commanding) in India. The planned route was via Paris, Rome, Malta, Cairo, Bagdad, and Karachi – 5,560 miles, accomplished in a time of 72 hours and 41 minutes, at an average speed of 77 mph. Only once did they land at their designated aerodrome on the flight plan. When they arrived in Delhi, the Viceroy, and a crowd of 30,000 greeted them.

The London *Daily Mail* was keenly interested in the great adventure. The following account was published:

"A British Aeroplane left England today, Friday (13 December 1918) for a flight to India.

At 9.30 a.m., a giant Handley Page, of V/1500 type, carrying six members of the Royal Air Force, rose from the aerodrome at Martlesham, near Ipswich, and headed for the Channel and France on a flight to Karachi, and hence to Delhi.

The huge craft crossed the Channel but ran into a bank of thick fog and was compelled to land at a small town near the French coast. It is hoped that the weather tomorrow morning will allow a continuance of the journey, and that Miramas, near Marseille, may be reached to-morrow night.

On the front of the engines was "H.M.A. Old Carthusian." She was named by chief pilot, Major Archibald Stuart McLaren, M.C., A.F.C., who was a Charterhouse boy, as was one of the passengers, General McEwen.

If everything goes well and the most sanguine of hopes are realised the journey may be made in seven stages.

A.F.C. – Pioneering Through Flight to India

As Halley later recalled in his lively account of the flight for Aeroplane Monthly (December 1978):

'It was indeed a great moment. MacLaren and I had a lot in common, except that he was 6ft. 2in. and I 5ft. 3in wearing my thick socks! He was also a Scot and had already flown to Egypt in an 0/400 with General "Biffy" Borton. Our considerable experience on heavy aircraft had brought us together … A day or two later we were at Martlesham Heath, as it was from there that we were going to start, and Rolls-Royce mechanics were working on the aircraft. All the crew were now assembled there. Flight Sergeant Smith and Sergeant Crockett, fitters, and Sergeant Brown, rigger, had been selected as maintenance crew. Going with us as a passenger was General Norman McEwan, who was to take over as A.O.C. in India on arrival. As General MacEwen and MacLaren were both at school at Charterhouse, the aircraft was named H.M.A. Old Carthusian. We also had another passenger, "Tiny", a little Maltese Terrier

belonging to MacLaren that had already flown to Egypt earlier in the year. He was mad keen on flying and whenever the engines started, he ran to the bottom of the ladder to be taken up into the cockpit!'

Thus ensued an extraordinary journey, via Paris, Rome, Malta, Cairo, Baghdad, and Karachi, the whole enacted between 13 December 1918 and 15 January 1919, a journey 'full of incidents, some of them not easy to cope with', not least the final flight into Karachi – Christopher Cole and Roderick Grant take up the story in But Not in Anger:

'To reduce weight only one of the N.C.O.s could travel – he was in fact needed in the tail cockpit to give the correct trim for take-off – and Smith won the toss. While Halley dashed back to get their kit and pay the bills, MacLaren taxied his way between the dunes as fast as he dared to avoid getting stuck in the soft sand. The tide was right out leaving a two-mile strip of firm, damp beach. There was a slope across its width, but the pair of sound engines was on the side to counteract any tendency to swing. Today, a three-engine ferry take-off by a four-engine aircraft from a concrete runway is a routine piece of operating procedure, and with the substantial power reserves of a modern jet transport presents no hazard. The crew of Old Carthusian were – as far as is known – doing it for the first time in aviation history, in a hot climate, from wet sand in an aircraft considered underpowered even by 1919 standards.

MacLaren opened up the three Eagles and at 17.45 the aircraft slowly rolled away, gradually picked up speed and was airborne after a run of about a mile. Twenty minutes later they had reached 1,000 feet and were passing the Britomart on their starboard side. Her smoke was still a smudge on the horizon when their justifiable elation was rudely shattered as both starboard engines gave a few splutters and then stopped, leaving them to defy gravity by the sole efforts of the front port. The crew's immediate diagnosis was the right one – the wind driven pump for transferring fuel from the main tank to the starboard gravity tank had finally shed all its miserable little vane cups and given up the struggle. Halley dived back to the engineer's station and strenuously attacked the emergency pump with both hands, wondering how he could attract Smith's attention. The engines picked up again and Halley hastened back to the cockpit. He had just managed to get through to Smith – 60 feet to the rear – by sign language when the engines again stopped, and again Halley rushed to the pumps. As the engines picked up for the second time, Smith came crawling down the fuselage and thereafter they took turns to man the pumps.

At 18.45, just as the last light had faded, and with about 35 miles to go the rear starboard engine began to lose revolutions, its temperature shot up and there was no alternative but to throttle it right down, then switch off completely. The seizure was due to a broken oil pipe, and nothing could be done in flight. Since they were providentially left with an engine on each side, they retained reasonable control though it was impossible to maintain height. The next half hour seemed like an eternity. With both remaining engines at full throttle and their temperatures reading only 5 degrees C below boiling point, MacLaren held the aircraft barely above the stall, and with the airspeed indicator showing 52 m.p.h. she staggered along, losing about 10 feet of vital altitude with every minute that passed. They just scraped over the ridge of hills to the west of Karachi, but very soon they must hit the ground and there was no possibility *of circling around looking for the city's temporary aerodrome.*

By some happy chance, the priority departure signal despatched by Brown from Ormara had not only arrived but was sent straight away by runner to the senior Royal Engineer officer who was playing hockey. He immediately appreciated the need for urgent action, grabbed some men and hastily improvised flares from petrol and rags, and for good measure fired off a few pyrotechnics as soon as the faint drone of engines was heard to the west. From the flight deck of Old Carthusian, the crew peered at the myriad lights of Karachi still some miles away and wondered where they could safely put down. Then Halley gave a wild shout and pointed straight ahead. He had spotted one of the signals, and faintly twinkling on the ground almost dead in line with their heading was an obvious flare-path. They were now frighteningly low down and the straight in approach had to be exactly right, first time. It was precisely so and when the Handley Page rolled to a halt at 19.15 the pilots climbed out, grabbed one another by the arms and literally danced for joy.

"Until that moment I thought that dancing for joy was just a figure of speech", recalls Halley, "but we did it – though since we were such an oddly sized couple, the onlookers probably thought we were quite mad. They had seen us make a good and apparently normal landing but knew nothing of our harrowing experience."

Present day jet passengers bothered by the effect of long-distance travel on their circadian rhythm or body clock may care to reflect that this first England to India flight over a distance of 5,560 miles was accomplished in 72 hours 41 minutes, at an average speed of 77mph

That night Halley underlined the impression that flyers were eccentric people by arriving for dinner with the Governor of Sind half an hour late and wearing a dinner suit nearly a foot too long in the sleeves and leg. He had fallen asleep in his bath from sheer fatigue – and was not the easiest to fit when it came to borrowing clothes.

When McEwen arrived and heard the full story, he promptly forestalled any criticism of the pilots by signalling Air Ministry, saying that he could not speak too highly of their enterprise, grit and determination for successfully completing the flight in the face of so many difficulties, particularly during the final 170 miles – over 50 of which there was no possibility of landing.

Despite only once being able to land at the aerodrome designated on their flight plan, the crew had nearly always managed to notify some authority of their whereabouts before anxiety was aroused. The aircraft was for a short time posted as missing after the forced landing in Egypt, since it had not been sighted after passing Sollum, and H.Q. Middle East was about to launch a major search when the message reporting its safety was received.'

The Viceroy of India later asked Halley to carry out a daring bombing strike on **Kabul**, Afghanistan. At 03.00 hours on 24 May 1919, *Old Carthusian* took off. The route was northwest towards the Khyber Pass, on up the Kabul River and followed a rough road to Jalalabad just as the sun was coming up. Then west another 90 miles to Kabul. They pressed on despite a starboard engine water leak coming from the second cylinder. The precipitous mountains ahead were the next concern, they just managed to clear the gap where the road went through the 8,000 feet ridge of Jagalak Pass.

Kabul Raid

Having then flown on to Delhi, where a crowd of 30,000 and the Viceroy greeted the Old Carthusian, and undertaken some V.I.P. flights, Halley was summoned by General McEwan in lieu of the mounting troubles on the frontier and, to cut a long story short, was ordered to carry out a daring bombing strike on Kabul. Halley takes up the story:

'Four 112lb. bomb racks from No. 31 Squadron's B.E.2Cs were attached to the lower wing main spars and connected to the front cockpit where an Observer would release the bombs. We put sixteen 20-pounders in the rear cockpit, and they would be dropped by the crew once the 112lb. bombs had been released. We had to true up the wings and tighten the fabric. We also fitted two laminated four-bladed propellers fashioned from a local wood called padouk.

We took off at about 3 a.m. on 24 May 1919 – Empire Day. An L-shaped flare path was laid out, consisting of seven flares made from empty five-gallon oil drums filled with oil-soaked cotton waste. These proved effective for take-off and would have been useful if it were found necessary to land in the dark in case of emergency.

The route lay towards the Khyber Pass, and as the clearing height was about 3,000 feet this meant flying around for about an hour to gain height before going over a ridge of hills. The Khyber was only dimly visible, as were a few lights at Jamrud Fort and Landi Kotal. From there we flew over the Kabul River and a rough road running parallel up to Jalalabad, the only town of any size on the route. As we were approaching Jalalabad and daybreak was coming up, I was checking the starboard rev. counter when to my horror I saw water leaking from the base of the second cylinder. I got Flight Sergeant Smith up beside me and, with engines throttled back to aid hearing, we hurriedly conferred as to what should be done.

The leak was caused by a defective rubber connection fitted between the water jacket and the collecting pipe running along the base of the six cylinders. Drops of water were being blown by the slipstream, making it impossible to estimate the extent of the leakage. Kabul was still about 90 miles ahead, and there was the return time to think about. I was in the middle of a steep turn, and on looking down noticed smoke from a fire being blown in the direction of Kabul and stretching out parallel with the ground, indicating a favourable wind of some force.

Villiers got Flight Sergeant Smith alongside me again, and after some shrugging of shoulders and other signs of an even chance, we decided to continue.

Oh, God – somewhere ahead there was that ridge to cross, with Kabul still further on. Much went through my mind at this stage of the journey. I was continually looking at the leakage and the frightening appearance of the precipitous mountains around. The Jagfalak Pass, through which the road went at nearly 8,000 feet, was not yet visible. It was quite thrilling threading one's way between high peaks. Suddenly on making a turn, the road appeared on a crest of the ridge ahead, but to my horror it was some height above the aircraft's nose.

Remembering the smoke, we had just left behind, I wondered whether we could gain enough up-lift to take us over the hills ahead. At about two miles away we were definitely below the ridge, so I said to myself "here goes" and, holding the nose up and with the four engines running full out we went sailing over the top and down on the other side. It was unbelievable – even now I can see the look Villiers had on his face! He quickly took to looking downwards from his side of the cockpit and with a grin gave me a "thumbs up"! Afterwards he told me that, on passing over the ridge, he saw a camel convoy of over 100 animals on its way to Kabul or the Khyber stampede in all directions, quite a number falling down the precipitous mountain side.

On getting over the ridge and regaining my breath I saw our target ahead, spread out over a vast area on a lush green fertile plateau; a marked change from the barren and mountainous terrain that we had just come across. With a population of 300,000, it was not surprising that Kabul covered such an area. It was also reputed to have the busiest and finest Bazaar in the East.

Owing to the risk of starboard engine failure, we had to cut our time over Kabul to a minimum. Nevertheless, the bombing achieved good results, and if that didn't frighten a city that had never seen an aircraft before, the sight and sound of the Old Carthusian roaring over the city at a few hundred feet with four engines fitted with stub exhausts certainly did!

On the return journey we again headed for the Jagdalak Pass, and believe it or not, had the benefit of a slightly following wind, which had veered through 180 degrees! As we were now relieved of our bombs, we flew over the ridge with height to spare.

The return flight seemed interminable, and we were all very conscious of the water leakage on the starboard engine. My eyes were glued to the temperature gauge in the nacelle, and we had nearly reached the Khyber when I saw the pointer rise slowly above normal; there was nothing to do but switch off the engine and carry on with three running full out to keep height. This we were able to do and landed at Risalpur after six hours in the air. It would be an understatement to say we were all greatly relieved!

The main object of bombing Kabul was to alarm King Amanullah, a result so successfully attained that a message came to the Viceroy immediately afterwards to the effect that the Afghans wanted peace. This was the end of the Old Carthusian's career, which had been bedevilled by misfortune from first to last. Nevertheless, the old V/1500 had accomplished something unique in history – it had ended a war on its own! So finished the Third Afghan War, terminated by a strategic bombing raid at a negligible cost which must have saved hundreds of lives and the cost of an extensive land campaign. It also restored peace to *a large slice of India.*

The raid had one or two amusing angles to it. For example, when Amanullah's uncle, a keen golfer, died suddenly under rather questionable circumstances, Amanullah had him buried under the first tee. As one of our twenty-pounders, carelessly thrown out by the crew, had landed near the grave, Amanullah complained to the Viceroy that we had bombed the tomb of his ancestor! Another comic episode appeared in The Aeroplane of 22 April 1942. The founding editor, C. G. Grey wrote, 'The raid on Kabul was made with decisive effect – that was when Jock Halley blew out the walls of the King's Harem and started the fashion of female emancipation in Afghanistan!'

A few years after the Afghan War, King Amanullah visited England as a guest, and was given an air display at Hendon. Being in Scotland at the time I was unable to attend. However, I received a letter from C. G. Grey: 'Dear Jock, I noticed you were conspicuous by your absence at Hendon on Saturday. Had you been there no doubt you would have had a knife in your back!'

There is one final comment that I would like to make concerning the raid. As the pilot and captain of the aircraft I was given a Second Bar to my Distinguished Flying Cross. However, my stalwart N.C.O.s, Flight Sergeant Smith and Sergeant Crockett, fitters, and Sergeant Brown, rigger, who accompanied me quite voluntarily and who had supervised the rebuilding of the aircraft, received no official recognition in spite of all my recommendations. They had all won the Air Force Medal for their efforts on the flight to India. Now, we know that the D.F.C. and D.F.M. are awarded for 'distinguished flying in the face of the enemy,' and the A.F.C. and A.F.M. for 'distinguished flying in the face of Providence!' Surely these brave men had earned some recognition in the former category and Lieutenant Villiers also.

Here, belatedly, let me pay my respects to them' (Aeroplane August 1979, refers).

'Old Carthusian' dropped 20 bombs, one 112-pound and three 20-pound on the Amir's palace sending the ladies of the royal harem into the streets screaming in terror, this caused a great scandal. Another three 112-pound and seven 20-pound bombs hit the royal arsenal at Arg causing a large explosion. Six hours later they landed at Risalpur, now in Pakistan.

King Amanullah had declared Jihad on 3 May 1919 and sent the 50,000 strong Afghan army supported by 120,000 frontier tribesmen into British India to start the Third Afghan War, known in Afghanistan as the War of Independence. The Treaty of Gandamak in 1879 had held for 40 years, but now they wanted to be free and independent of existing treaties with British India.

The purpose of the Halley raid was to alarm King Amanullah and it did so successfully, attaining an immediate message to the Viceroy in India that the Afghans wanted peace. Halley later claimed to have 'ended the war on his own'. An armistice was signed on 8 August 1919.

D.F.C. London Gazette 3 August 1918:

'A gallant and determined leader in long distance night bombing raiding. He has been most successful in many of these raids, generally under adverse weather conditions and intense anti-aircraft fire from the enemy and having had to fly by compass owing to density of mist. In his last raid the flight outward and homeward lasted eight hours.'

Later Years

Gaining steady promotion between the Wars, Halley enjoyed varied employment, including stints with the Fleet Air Arm in *HMS Eagle* and *HMS Glorious.* in the 1920s and 1930s. He was Assistant Commandant at RAF Cranwell when WW2 started. He was posted to Gibraltar as Commanding Officer of No. 200 Group, Coastal Command in 1941. Halley pressed the Governor, Lord Gort, to back his plan for extending the runway to deal with "modern aircraft", a plan which in fact the Governor refused to support, instead complaining to the C.-in-C. Coastal Command about Halley. He was ordered back to RAF Silloth in Cumbria as Station Commander. Inevitably, the Gibraltar runway was extended in time for "Operation Torch", the North African landings on 8 November 1942.

Group Captain Robert Halley DFC & 2 Bars, AFC (Air Force Cross) was made a Wing Commander on 1 July 1933 and Group Captain on 1 July 1938. He retired from the RAF on 6 May 1945. Group Captain Robert Halley died on 13 December 1979, exactly 61 years since his departure to India. His obituary stated that he was 'one of the aviation 'greats' of all time, a man cast in the 'heroic mould'.

Awards:

Bar to D.F.C. London Gazette 1 January 1919.

Second Bar to D.F.C. London Gazette 12 July 1920 (Afghanistan).

A.F.C. London Gazette 22 December 1919.

First and Second D.F.C.s – Night Bomber Pilot

Medals

In September 2011, the medals of Group Captain Robert Halley were sold by auction. Established in 1990, Dix Noonan Webb Ltd are the UK's leading specialist auctioneers and valuers of banknotes, coins, tokens, medals, and militaria staging regular auctions throughout the year.

The following information is from the information provided by Dix Noonan Webb at the time of sale of the medals.

Robert Halley's medal were sold by auction with a quantity of original documentation, including the recipient's original Royal Naval Air Service Pilot's Flying Logbook, covering the period February 1917 until September 1919, and two or three portrait photographs, together with a letter opener fashioned from wood taken from one of the Old Carthusian's propellers, with ink inscription and Halley's signature:

copies of Aeroplane Monthly for December 1978 (with Halley's account of the U.K. to India flight), August 1979 (with his account of the Kabul raid), and November 1979 (with his account of Hendon displays in the 1920s); and bound photocopies of the A.O.C. India's official report on the U.K. to India flight and the text of a speech given by Halley on the same subject; so, too, a CD from the Royal Air Force Museum's film and sound archive, with an interview with Halley.

Dix Noonan Webb Ltd.

LONDON SPECIALIST AUCTIONEERS

Lot 912

Date of Auction: 23rd September 2011

Sold for £24,000

Estimate: £18,000 – £20,000

The unique Great War and Afghan War D.F.C. and 2 Bars, A.F.C. group of eleven awarded to Group Captain R. "Jock" Halley, Royal Air Force, late Royal Naval Air Service: having won a brace of D.F.C.s for his gallantry in daring long-distance night bombing raids to Germany in 1918, he was awarded the A.F.C. for the epic flight of the Super Handley V/1500 Old Carthusian to India – where he promptly won a third D.F.C. for a remarkable raid on Kabul in May 1919.

Distinguished Flying Cross, G.V.R., with Second and Third Award Bars, unnamed as issued; Air Force Cross, G.V.R., unnamed as issued; British War and Victory Medals, M.I.D. oak leaf (Capt. R. Halley, R.A.F.); India General Service 1908-35, 1 clasp, Afghanistan N.W.F. 1919 (Flt. Lieut. R. Halley, R.A.F.); 1939-45 Star; Africa Star; Defence and War Medals, M.I.D. oak leaf; Jubilee 1935; Coronation 1937, mounted court-style as worn, very fine and better – £18000-22000

Notes:

RNASTE (Royal Naval Air Service Training Establishment) Vendôme was located between Le Mans and Orléans.

Bobby Reece originally served with the *La Lafayette Escadrille*. The escadrille of the *Aéronautique Militaire* was composed largely of American volunteer pilots flying fighters. Bobby Reece came over from the USA and joined the "Lafayette" in 1915. Reece apparently crashed so many planes that they let him go. Halley described Reece as 'ham-handed' as a pilot but had managed to wrangle his way into becoming his observer in RAF 216 Squadron. Bobby Reece was awarded the DFC at the same time as Robert Halley during a bombing mission to Germany, one of the few Americans to hold this award. Reece was part of the Reece Buttonhole Manufacturing Company, Sewing Machine Manufacturers, Boston Massachusetts, USA. The company is still in business, merging with AMF Sewn Products Inc. in 1991 to form AMF Reece.

The airfield at Risalpur was created in 1910 by the Royal Flying Corp. RFC/RAF No. 31 Squadron flew B.E.2c and Farman biplanes in a ground support role from Risalpur. In 1947, it became the airfield of the Pakistan Air Force (PAF). In 1967 it was upgraded to the Pakistan Air Force Academy Asghar Khan.

On 17 May 1919, a Handley Page Type O/400, D5439 of RAF 58 Squadron carrying Thomas Edward Lawrence (Lawrence of Arabia) on a flight to Cairo, Egypt crashed at the airport of Roma-Centocelle. T E Lawrence had been attending the 1919 Peace Conference in Paris and had hitched a ride in order to collect from Cairo documents relating to his service in the Middle East during the Great War. The pilot and co-pilot were both killed; Lawrence survived the incident with a broken shoulder blade and two broken ribs. The latter injury troubling him for the rest of his life.

Captain John William Alcock DSC and Lieutenant Arthur Whitten Brown of the RAF aboard Vickers Vimy F.B.27A Mk.IV biplane bomber made the very first successful non-stop trans-Atlantic crossing by air on 14-15 June 1919

A Bristol Fighter, **BF4626** aeroplane of RAF 20 Squadron was lost on 30 July 1919 during the conflict. Acting Captain George Eastwood was shot through the chest by a party of tribesmen concealed on the hillside. The observer, 2nd Lieutenant David Lapraik was also injured. A rescue mission was undertaken by the Kurram Militia from the post at Badama. Both airmen survived, George Eastwood was discharged from the RAF in December 1919 and David Lapraik in May 1920.

In December 1978, **Aeroplane Monthly** published the first-hand account of Group Captain Robert Halley's trail-blazing journey to India at the end of 1918. This magazine article is still under copyright, but a back issue may still be available to purchase and some of the text was reprinted when Halley's medals were auctioned in 2011.

Titled: **Per Ardua Ad India**

Subtitle: Sixty years ago, on December 13, 1918, the third prototype Handley Page V/1500, J1936, took off from Martlesham Heath for a flight to India. GP CAPT ROBERT HALLEY, AFC now aged 63, was one of the pilots, and he recalls this trail-blazing through flight from England to India, a journey bedevilled by bad weather and mechanical failures

Opening Text: '*On Friday, December 13, 1918, the second aircraft to fly to India from this country took off from Martlesham Heath in Suffolk. As I happened to be the co-pilot, along with Maj. Stuart MacLaren, on that early pioneer flight, and this year – 1978, a record of some of the amusing things that happened, together with some of the rather frightening occurrences with which we had to cope, might be of interest.*'

Closing Text: '*We had left on Friday, December 13th, 1918, and arrived on January 15, 1919 – and we never once landed at out intended destination! Up to this time I had never been a superstitious man, but after all we went through, I am still inclined to look a little askance at Friday the 13th.*'

Group Captain Robert Halley

Picture – Ron Eisele

Aerial view of part of Kabul taken from Handley Page V/1500, J1936, "HMA Old Carthusian", during its bombing raid on the Afghan capital, 24 May 1919Attribution: British Air Force RAF, Public domain, via Wikimedia Commons

https://upload.wikimedia.org/wikipedia/commons/1/15/Aerial_photography_during_bombing_raid_on _Kaul_Afghanistan_24_May_1919.jpg

Picture – Ron Eisele

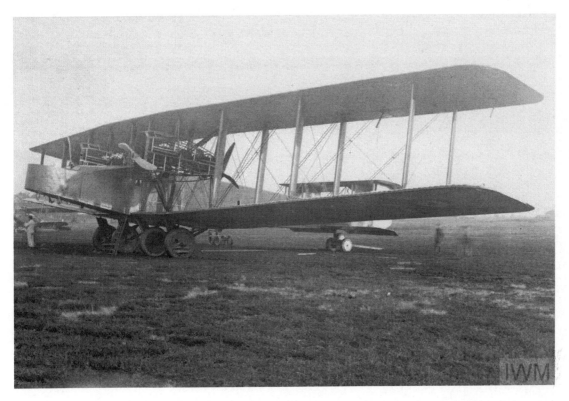

BRITISH AIRCRAFT OF THE FIRST WORLD WAR (Q 68142) Handley Page V/1500-night heavy bomber.
Copyright: © IWM. Original Source: http://www.iwm.org.uk/collections/item/object/205315435

BRITISH AIRCRAFT IN THE FIRST WORLD WAR (Q 67636) Handley Page V/1500 heavy bomber biplane.
Copyright: © IWM. Original Source: http://www.iwm.org.uk/collections/item/object/205184431

BRITISH AIRCRAFT OF THE FIRST WORLD WAR (Q 68142) Handley Page V/1500-night heavy bomber. Copyright: © IWM. Original Source: http://www.iwm.org.uk/collections/item/object/205315435

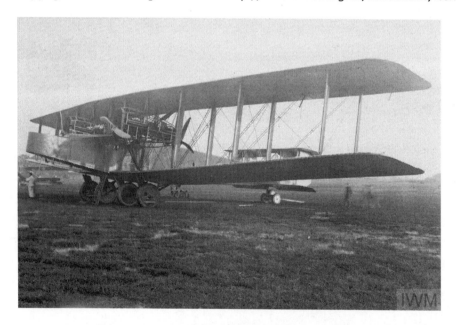

AIRCRAFT OF THE ROYAL AIR FORCE 1918-1939 (H(AM) 194) A Handley Page V/1500 bomber, which made the first flight from England to India in January 1919. In May 1919 it bombed rebel Afghans in Kabul and was thus the only V/1500 to see action. Copyright: © IWM. Original Source: http://www.iwm.org.uk/collections/item/object/205125510

7 John William Dunne

Those Magnificent Men in their Flying Machines, yes, they went up tiddly up and down tiddly down in would you believe in the Highlands of Perthshire. It may surprise you to learn that the War Office had to put out a statement in 1907 dismissing rumours that the Balloon Factory near Farnborough Common was to be transferred to some remote spot in the vicinity of Dunkeld. The reason being, that during tests of new military airships at the Royal Aircraft Establishment, Farnborough, the crowds were so great, and the photographers so persistent, that some quieter spot was imperatively necessary, if indiscreet and secret revelations were not to be made.

On 5 October 1907, the first British flight by a powered airship, British Army Dirigible, *Nulli Secundus* flew from Farnborough to Crystal Palace in London. It was piloted by Samuael Franklin Cody with Colonel J. E. Capper on board.

A small working party of Royal Engineers from the Army Balloon Factory was sent northwards to conduct certain work in connection with the fitting of machinery to a new airship, but not to Dunkeld, the out-of-the-way spot was in fact on the Duke of Atholl's estate at Blair Atholl. These top-secret tests they hoped would lead to the first engine powered British military aeroplane.

A delicate aircraft was put in a railway carriage at Farnborough in July 1907 and transported under great secrecy up to Blair Atholl, then carted from the station up to Glen Tilt, just north of the village. Here the aircraft was assembled and camouflaged from inquisitive eyes by having white stripes and dark patches painted on the upper surfaces.

The aircraft design was of a swept back arrowhead planform design with no movable vertical surfaces. Starting with the glider, Dunne D.1-A, the aircraft configuration was tested at Glen Tilt, launched from a 4-wheel trolley and flown by Colonel Capper, it achieved some success, but was heavily damaged on landing, hitting a wall. Repaired and brought closer to Blair Atholl, power was added to it with two 12hp Buchet engines. The now modified John William Dunne designed aircraft; the D.1-B, piloted by Lieutenant Lancelot Gibbs, first for one successful 8-second flight on 29 September 1907. It was again either damaged on landing wrecked when it rolled off the chassis of the trolley gear. This was not an uncommon event in the early days of flying.

Certain parts of the test aeroplane were sent the next day by train to Farnborough for minor alterations and repairs. They were packed at daybreak and loaded onto two railways wagons ready to be attached to the afternoon express from Inverness.

These experiments had validated the stability Dunne considered so indispensable to flight. Dunne had concentrated his efforts on tailless designs, and he produced inherently stable aircraft, capable of flying steadily, even with the controls locked on a straight course, all by itself.

In 1905, Dunne had been appointed to the Army Balloon Factory at South Farnborough, England, then under the competent leadership of Colonel John Edward Capper. Capper was the pilot of the Dunne aircraft and was slightly injured in the glider flight

The Marquis of Tullibardine (heir to the Duke of Atholl) told the press in an interview that everything pointed to success. *"Even if people like myself, who are sceptical concerning the utility of these things as fighting machines, have been convinced. Personally, and in common with many other soldiers, I would rather they were unnecessary, but while other nations are at work on them it would be poor tactics for Great Britain to lag behind. Lieutenant Dunne wishes his inventions to be at the disposal of the British Government, he is actuated purely by patriotic motives. I have ascertained that the model tested in the valley of the Tilt will glide, drive, or hover, and that stability in a marvellous degree has been attained."*

The Marquis also spoke of the loyalty of his retainers, "the gillies have been without sleep night after night and have questioned everyone who lingered on the road. They are trained men, and even the shepherds can signal by semaphore." The popular recounting of Dunne's flying episode asserts that such great clandestineness was observed that "the [Duke's] tenants were enrolled as a sort of bodyguard to prevent unauthorized persons from entering".

John William Dunne was born at the Curragh Camp in County Kildare, Ireland, on 2 December 1875. He became a soldier at the outbreak of the Second Boer War and volunteered for the Imperial Yeomanry as an ordinary Trooper fighting in South Africa. In 1900 he was caught up in an epidemic of typhoid fever and was invalided home. He recovered and was commissioned as a Second Lieutenant in the Wiltshire's. He went back to South Africa in March 1902, and he again fell ill, diagnosed with heart disease. He was again invalided home.

It was then that Dunne instigated his study of the science of aerodynamics and flight in earnest, commencing with observations of avian flight and the *Alsomitra macrocarpa*, the seed of the Javan cucumber, also known as the Zanonia. A Zanonia seed is swept-winged and displays an inherent stability when dispersed by the wind. He became convinced that a safe aeroplane needed to have inherent aerodynamic stability.

Dunne growing up was inspired by a Jules Verne story at the age of 13, he envisaged a machine that could fly, one that did not require steering, that would right itself irrespective of wind or weather. Fortified by the encouragement of a family friend, the writer of science fiction H. G. Wells, Dunne designed and built a number of prototypes based on a 'tailless' design. At that time when Dunne first took up the study of aviation, no one had yet flown in Europe, and he could therefore receive little benefit from the results achieved by other pilots and constructors.

The test flying at Blair Atholl was five years, almost to the day, since the Wright Brothers' epic flight travelled almost the same distance at Kill Devil Hills, Kitty Hawk, North Carolina USA. Preston Watson had also been attempting to get off the ground with his designs since the summer of 1903 at Erroll, and later in 1909 at Forgandenny. Frank and Harold Barnwell were experimenting at the same time at Causeway Head, just below the Wallace Monument. They managed to achieve a flight of just 80 yards on 28 July 1909, this was regarded as the first successful powered flight in Scotland. A year later they flew for one mile, again at Causewayhead. In France, Santos Dumont, the Brazilian aviation innovator, had been astonishing the world in 1906 with his flying feats at the Château de Bagatelle near Paris and on 25 July 1909, Louis Charles Joseph Blériot crossed the English Channel, landing at Northfall Meadow, close to Dover Castle.

In the spring of 1909, the War Office support for Dunne's airplane development was withdrawn. Dunne left the Balloon Factory, taking the D.4 with him. He continued his work under the aegis of the Blair Atholl Aeroplane Syndicate Ltd., formed in 1910 by the Marquis of Tullibardine. Like its predecessor, the D.4 was camouflaged, it was fitted with two 15hp Buchet engines and later a single 25hp R.E.P. engine. Dunne regarded the D.4 as 'more of a hopper than a flier'. The best flight of the D.4 was 120 feet (36.58m) on 10 December 1908.

In 1910 the Dunne designed aircraft D.5, built by Short Brothers, was demonstrated on a flying field at Eastchurch, Isle of Sheppey. The same airfield that five years later, 30 June 1915, Preston Watson took off from on his final flight. He crashed and died 20 miles from his destination at Eastbourne. Charles Richard Fairey became the General manager of the Blair Atholl Syndicate at Eastchurch, working with Dunne on his tailless aircraft. A Fairey Gannet, carrier-bourne aircraft sat outside at Erroll airfield for many years. The Gannet featured a tricycle undercarriage, a feature pioneered by John William Dunne and others in that early pioneer era of aviation.

John William Dunne was not only a pioneering aeronautical engineer, but he was also a philosopher and the author of, An Experiment with Time in 1927. A treatise on precognition, consciousness, and the concept of time. Dunne argued that past, present, and future were in fact simultaneous and only experienced sequentially because of our mental perception of them. Dunne also published a book on dry-fly fishing: Sunshine and the Dry Fly in 1924, discussing a new method of making realistic artificial flies.

Dunne vision of tailless aircraft design was finally realised with the construction of 'flying wings', such as the 1920s' Westland Pterodactyl, which Dunne helped design, the 1929 Waldo Waterman Whatsit, the 1940s' Northrup Flying Wing, and the modern stealth aircraft like the Northrop Grumman B-2. This aviation legend also pioneered many other aircraft features which were not destined to reappear for many years.

John William Dunne FRAeS (1875–1949) died at Banbury in England on 24 August 1949, aged 74.

Notes:

There was much concern from local Perthshire folk about the operations at Blair Atholl in 1907 and this perhaps ingrained in them for many years after an irrational fear of being attacked whilst they slept. In October of 1914 in Pitlochry many observers of the western sky wondered for the fourth night in a row, what were the mysterious various coloured light flashes in the sky. It was first reported by Pitlochry Police Sergeant, Cameron and ex-Sergeant Grant. This visitant it was conjectured might be the long-threatened Zeppelin airship raid. The unusual light show in the sky usually lasted for about thirty minutes, then receded northward. This same light show event was also reported further south in Cheshire, England.

This was not the first occurrence of this in Pitlochry, in March of 1913 a bright light described as being "like the moon with a haze over it." This incident went unreported at the time, and it was later suggested that it was the northward flight of some mysterious phantom aircraft. A similar sighting was reported on the same night in Kirkcaldy and Montrose.

The nearest Zeppelin airship bombing attack to Perthshire, was on the night of 2/3 May 1916, it was just west of Arbroath and again just north of Carnoustie. One of two attacking Zeppelins then proceeded north hoping to find a target in the Cromarty Firth. It managed to get itself lost in bad weather and they found themselves over Loch Ness. It gave up and reversed course until it was over Aberdeenshire where it released six bombs on a mansion house near Rhynie, mistaking it for a coal mine. The owners had neglected to turn off their newly installed electric lights. A few more bombs were dropped before it made its way out to sea. Not having enough fuel to return to Germany, it headed for neutral Norway.

Experimental Aircraft Designed by John William Dunne

D.1-A Glider. Built in 1907 – limited success in a single flight.

D.1-B Powered Airplane (modified D.1-A). Built in 1907 – crashed during its first flight.

D.2 Training Glider. Designed in 1907 – never constructed.

Dunne-Huntington. Gas Powered Triplane.

Designed in 1907/8 - flown successfully in 1911.

D.3 Person-carrying Glider. Flown successfully in 1908.

D.4 Powered Airplane. Flown in 1908 – partially successful

(in Dunne's words, "more a hopper than a flyer").

D.5 Powered tailless biplane. Flown successfully in 1910.

D.6 Monoplane. Built in 1911 – never flown.

D.7 Monoplane. Built in 1911 – flown successfully.

D.8 Biplane. Several built and flown in 1912-13.

D.9 Sesquiplane. Begun in 1913 – never fully constructed.

D.10 Biplane. Built in 1913 – a complete failure.

John William Dunne

John William Dunne, D.5, Eastchurch 14 June 1910

Dunne D.1-A/ D.1-B, 1907 Glen Tilt

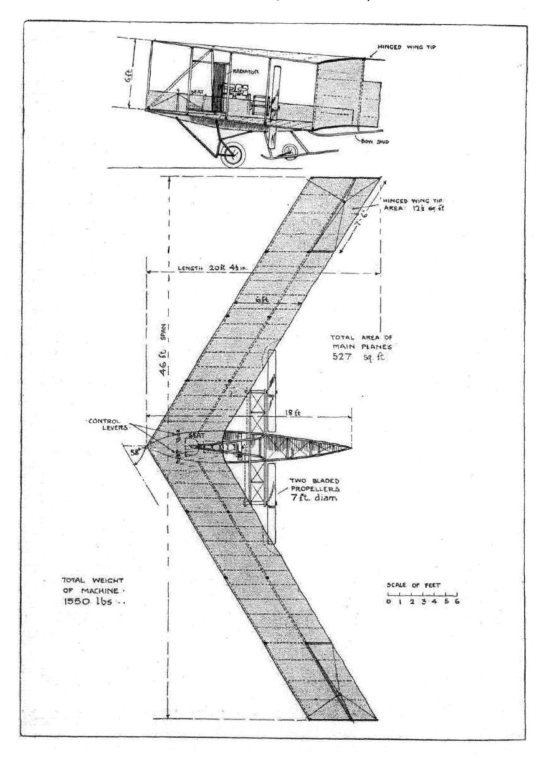

Dunne D.5, published in Flight magazine June 1910

8 Jessie Jordan

The story of Jessie Jordan has been told many times, in books and newspaper articles, but few know of her Perth connections and her complicated life. What was the reason for doing what she did by turning traitor against the country of her birth? Perhaps the story of her life may put some light on her betrayal of her own people.

Jessie had a hard life; she was unlucky in love and perhaps this made her into a toughened-by-life survivor. Jessie's father was William Ferguson who abandoned her and Jessie's mother when he left for Canada. Jessie' mother was Elizabeth Wallace, a domestic servant from the village of Calder near Coatbridge. Jessie's birth certificate states that she was born illegitimate on 23 December 1887 at 1.50am in a Maternity Hospital in Glasgow and was domiciled at Dixon's Rows, Calder. Dixon's Rows (or Raws) were small miner's houses consisting of 8 streets totalling 340 houses. Construction of the houses was stated in 1872 and they were privately owned by a local businessman, who was connected to the owners of the mining collieries in Blantyre, the Dixon family.

These houses were essentially hovels, not really fit for a family to live in. They were built of brick and had wooden shutters to close over the windows at night. Some houses may have had earthen floors, but most it is thought had a floor of flagstones. Cooking was done over an open fire, there was no sink or plumbing of any kind and some of the houses only had one room. Water was supplied from September of 1984, but only from a shared standpipe outside.

Following a miner's strike in April and May of 1874, Dixon's evicted its tenants from Dixon Rows and about 500 people ended up looking for shelter. Worse was to come in 1877 when the Blantyre Mining Disaster at Dixon's Collieries took the lives of over 200 men and boys. The community was effectively wiped out and the colliery owners Dixon's, again famously evicted all the widows and families from the houses as they were all tied to the deceased employees.

Jessie was taken straight from the maternity hospital to live with her grandmother. Jessie's own account states that she was an unwanted child but comfortable and happy with her granny.

Jessie's life must have improved somewhat you would think when her mother married John Haddow from Lanark. John Haddow was a widower with two sons. John Haddow was 30 years senior to Jessie's mother and had been married twice before. The family moved through to Perth, Jessie who was by that time about four or five years old. They stayed at 23 Friar Street in the Craigie district of Perth. By the time of the 1901 census, the family had grown, four sons and two daughters were listed. John Haddow was recorded as a Railway Engine Driver, and an elder son was shown employed as a Vanman.

Jessie's mother, according to Jessie, scared of John Haddow. Jessie recalled that her life was by now "sheer hell on earth", one of much unhappiness and that she was the recipient of many thrashings. She rarely went to school as her mother always had other things for her to do. She was only good at sewing and knitting; a teacher taught her dressmaking. She was proud that her work was shown at the Glasgow International Exhibition of 1901. Travelling incognito, the exhibition was visited by the King of Siam and Empress Eugenia, the wife of Napoleon III (granddaughter of William Kilpatrick of Malaga and Conheath. The Kilpatrick's of Dumfriesshire had settled in Spain as merchants in the 1730's. William was the U.S. Consul in Malaga (1800 - 1817).

Jessie attended The Western District School just along the street from where she lived. The Western District later became Craigie Primary School. It my guess that Jessie left school at 14 or 15. She decided she had had enough of her home life and left home. Her first position was as a house maid in a big house at the top of Kinnoull Hill

After about a year Jessie left this position and went to live with her grandmother in Motherwell. She grew tired of living with her relatives and wanted to move on, an opportunity arose to work for a Russian family who had a big house on the shores of the Gare Loch. Next, she was off to the Isle of Man to work the holiday season and then she was offered help in finding a job in Manchester by an elderly man staying at the hotel where she worked. Reality next dawned on the young, inexperienced, and naive Jessie of what scheming men really wanted and she decided her only option was to return to domestic service. She did have one more go at having a go as a dressmaker but another man that was staying at her digs offered her friendship but wanted her to go on the streets to make money for him. She cleared out and found a job as a maid in the Queen's Hotel in Manchester.

It was a good job but after a time her bad luck caught up with her. She fell down some stairs onto her head and sustained concussion. Three months were spent in hospital where she could not remember anything, she had lost her memory. On discharge from hospital, the doctors ordered her to take a holiday which she paid for with her compensation money. Jessie decided to go to Edinburgh and seeing that dressmaking was not for her she paid for a course of private lessons in hairdressing from a school in Princess Street. When this finished, she went to work for an Edinburgh lady as a maid.

After a few months had passed, Jessie decided to go and visit her mother. At this time, she thought her mother was now living in Falkirk with her husband, but they had been transferred to Dundee. In Dundee, Jessie found the love of her life. One day as she was going for something to eat at the Royal Hotel in Union Street, she met a young man coming down the stairs, crying. The young man was Frederick Jordan who was working as a waiter at the hotel and had just been informed that his brother had died in an accident in England.

Frederick knew little English, but Jessie found out that he wanted to go to the station. Jessie offered to take him there and, on the way, he asked for her name and address in order that he could write to her, to thank her for her kindness. Much to Jessie's surprise and delight she received a letter from him, just as he had promised. Jessie had returned to her job as a maid in Edinburgh. This was the start of a correspondence that lasted six months until the day Frederick intimated that he was coming to see her.

Frederick's parents, when he got back to Germany were against him returning to Britain. They had already lost one son and did not want another. Within a month or two he won them over and he could send for Jessie to come and stay with them in Hanover for a holiday. That holiday ended up lasting a year, by which time Jessie spoke German like a native.

Jessie met English ladies there and went out a lot. One English lady she met, lived permanently in Germany, was rich and had many influential friends. Jessie was to be surprised much later when the first World War broke out, that she was thought to be a British spy. Frederick had gone to work in France and Italy and after about a year, Jessie decided she would like another change. This lady, the supposed spy found her a position as a companion to a young lady who was being sent to East Africa. The young lady was pregnant and unmarried, it was to avoid a scandal.

After a year, Jessie returned to Germany, but Frederick was still away. She was recommended to a position with an American lady whose husband, a major in the German Army was away with the army. They transferred to Metz, but the place, Jessie described, was cold and dirty and it made her ill. Jessie continued to work, first taking a year off to recover from an illness. Then she took up another position as a companion to a lady in Hanover. She stayed with them a year and then had a holiday with them in Paris and Rouen.

During all this time Jessie had been in constant correspondence with Frederick. Jessie thought it was time to announce their engagement and this thought had occurred to his parents as well. Frederick was earning big money, so much it was thought he could retire in about ten years.

Jessie could have continued working, she was in fact asked to return to East Africa, but Frederick persuaded her not to go. They were married in Hamburg on 20 August 1912. A civil marriage first and then a religious ceremony in the Michaelis Church, the biggest in Hamburg at the time. They took up house in Hamburg and planned beautiful things for their life together - houses, cars, dresses, and travel.

A daughter was born, Marga on 18 May 1914. Her full name was Margaretta Frieda Wilhelmina, the last name being given as a token of loyalty to Kaiser Wilhelm, the last German Emperor. Three months later war broke out and Frederick was called up for military duty in one of their infantry regiments on 4 August 1914. Jessie shut up her house in Hamburg and with Marga moved in with Fredericks parents in Hannover.

Fredericks visits whilst on leave were joyous times for Jessie, but a double blow was about to strike. The war ended and Jessie got word that Frederick was returning home. Then two days later a second telegram arrived saying at what time he was coming. The next morning, another telegram came to say he was ill, and another the same night another to say that he was dead. The blow was so terrific that she recalled that she became lame, and that lasted for 6 months. When Frederick died is not known, there is a report that he succumbed to pneumonia after all the years in the trenches.

Jessie and her daughter returned to their home in Hamburg and three months later, Fredericks personal belongings arrived from the army. Then she recalled in her own words, the worst blow of her life fell. In the personal belongings were love letters to another woman that Frederick had been writing to, that he had met during training. This was a terrible blow, in secret she said that she cried and cried until she nearly made herself ill again.

The English lady, Jessie had a past friendship with, helped by giving her introductions to people and Jessie was soon in business visiting her clients giving beauty treatments. From then until 1919 Jessie had a lucrative business and was doing quite well, however it was a trying time for her socially and it was getting worse. She was British born and had become a German national by marriage, those who knew this seemed to go out of their way to be nasty to her. She was easily spotted as a foreigner as her speaking of German was not that of a natural born speaker. At a doctor's clinic she was jostled away from getting her child attended to. Her landlord wanted her out simply because she was British. He was persistent, so she took him to court to plead her case. Someone in the court shouted "Don't believe her! She's British and the British don't tell the truth." They were predisposed against all Britons, and they even suspected that she might be a British spy.

During the war, her faithless husband had met a Scotsman who forwarded a letter to Jessie's mother, who was now back living in Perth, saying that she was well. Jessie had not communicated with her mother in all the time she was in Germany. Jessie's mother wrote to Jessie in 1919 and asked her to return to her homeland. With no real plans for her future, she gave up her business and set sail with Marga for Leith.

Jessie thought that she might now stay in Scotland for good. It was not to be, her mother, husband and grandmother were all staying in Perth, but something was wrong. Her mother who she had not seen for twelve years left the house the minute Jessie arrived and did not come back for hours. She had a lover; a man Jessie had known from when she stayed in Perth before. When visiting, Jessie let slip something unintentionally. She did not know what she had said wrong, but it caused a terrible row.

Whilst staying in Perth, Jessie received a telegram from her mother-in-law saying that Herr Jordan, who she was very fond of, had died. Another awful blow as she said, that played havoc with her life. Jessie burst out crying which her mother, who was there at the time had never seen her do.

Something Jessie hated about her mother was the way that she was always watching her, just like she was back in Germany where they though she was a spy. Jessie stayed in Perth all the time she was there, her mother knew every move she made, everyone she visited and everything she did. Jessie could stand it no longer and overturned her decision to make Scotland her permanent home. At least she got love and attention from Frau Jordan, if from few others.

But how to get back, "that was the rub" she said. Jessie had no money and could not think of a way and then she remembered the present of a brooch from her husband. So, she parted with the brooch and used the money to book passage back to Germany for herself and Marga. Before leaving Jessie wrote to Frau Jordan telling her of her intention and to meet her at the docks in Hamburg. They lived together in Hamburg for the next six months. Shortly after returning she learned that her mother and the man who was her lover, had left Perth for Canada.

In 1920 Jessie married Baur Baumgarten, a wealthy Jewish merchant. It did not work out; he had an eye for other women. Jessie eventually divorced him in 1937 additionally caused by other factors coming into play. A significant number of her customers at her hairdressing and massage parlour in Germany were Jewish. The growth of Nazi-driven antisemitism in 1930's Germany contributed to a decline in Jessie's fortunes. Jessie was asked by the Nazi regime to prove that she and her daughter were 'Aryan' descent. The only way she had of proving that was by returning to Scotland and obtaining the necessary birth certificates and documents.

Just before leaving Hamburg, in February 1937, Jessie was approached by the German Abwehr secret police and invited to verify some information for them. Jessie later said they she bore no ill-will to Britain or had become pro-German. She just wanted to oblige German friends and because it would afford some excitement.

Arriving back in Perth, Jessie helped her stepbrother William who had recently lost his wife. William stayed at 16 Breadalbane Terrace, Friarton and it was from her that Jessie would start her new career as a spy.

Jessie's first espionage mission was to make drawings of the Royal Armament Depot at Rosyth dockyard. Taking along her nephew with her, they took the train from Perth to Dunfermline and then took a bus to the village of Charlestown, which overlooks the dockyard. Finding a suitable spot, Jessie started drawing. But Jessie's drawing skills were not very good, her handlers found that her drawings were of little use.

Jessie and her nephew next travelled down to North Wales where she left him in the care of an aunt, whilst she went off on another spying mission. This time with a camera she had purchased, she travelled down to Southampton and took pictures of the docks. On the way back to Wales she managed to wander about unchallenged at Aldershot Barracks taking more pictures.

Living in Perth was she felt, was too far away from the coast where most of her spying activities would take place. She needed to be closer to the places she would report on, so she bought a hairdressing shop at 1 Kinloch Street in Dundee. The shop was located near the top of the Hilltown and from here she would have a panoramic view of the comings and goings at the mouth of the River Tay and the docks in Dundee.

Once settled, Jessie resumed her espionage activities on the pretext of taking her nieces and nephews on seaside excursions, she visited all the coastal towns from Montrose down to Berwick, recording all the defence installations.

The German Abwehr decided that she would have another role, that of intermediary for correspondence between their agents in the US and Germany. The British Secret Service had by now been suspicious and were monitoring her mail. One letter she received that was intercepted was about a US Spy Ring, MI5 forwarded the information to the FBI. As a result, a plot to steal a defence map of the US East coast was averted and many German spies were arrested. Hollywood made a movie about this event in 1939 staring Edward G. Robinson, the Confessions of a Nazi Spy. The opening scene is of a

Scottish town with the postie delivering mail to a Mrs McLaughlin (aka Jessie Jordan) in Cathcart Road, Argyll, Scotland.

Jessie was eventually arrested and spent time awaiting trial in Perth Prison and Edinburgh's Saughton Prison. Jessie was found guilty of espionage, sentenced to four years penal servitude. One last tragedy for Jessie occurred whilst in prison, this was the loss of her daughter, still in Germany, in 1938, perhaps it is thought in a German hospital or perhaps while imprisoned there.

Jessie's good behaviour led her to being released early in 1941. Her freedom would not last long, she was immediately arrested and interned as an enemy alien.

Jessie remained interned for the rest of the war before returning to Germany when the war ended. Jessie died in Hamburg in 1954.

Notes:

The Jessie Jordan Perth connection started when I first noticed an envelope with a Breadalbane Terrace address in The National Archives, Kew documents that were released for public viewing on 26 August 2011. The Kew archive description was - Mrs Jessie JORDAN, alias WALLACE: German. Based in Perth, she acted as a recipient of intelligence for forwarding to the Abwehr. Correspondence with US Attaché arising from the American side of the case

So, two things got my attention, a Perth address on an envelope and why did they say she was based in Perth, and why on earth would she spy for the Germans. I decided to look at her earlier life to see where she came from and who were here parents.

Jessie was notorious at the time, and she was caught before WWII commenced. Was she foolish or manipulated, given that quite several British citizens were sympathetic to the German cause, she was perhaps not alone in being guilty? Jessie had a hard life, was unlucky in love, perhaps she was a toughened-by-life-survivor. Perhaps she felt unloved and unwanted, sought attention and found fulfilment by spying for the Nazi's in the lead up to WW2.

Page 10—SUNDAY MAIL, JUNE 12. 1938

My Amazing Life . . . . By Mrs. Jordan

I MAKE SKETCH IN FIFE ON GERMAN ORDERS

AS I wrote last Sunday, I was now approaching the most dangerous and exciting period of my life. I was about to become a spy in the interests of Germany. Maybe I had better say, here and now, that I did not take this step because I bore Britain any ill-will or had become pro-German.

Marga, Mrs. Jordan's daughter—a happy holiday snap.

Nothing is further from the truth.

I only did it to oblige friends in Germany, and because I felt it would afford some excitement. Excitement and change, as I have already shown, were like blood to me.

As my Counsel, Mr. A. P. Duffes, said in the High Court of Justiciary, what I did was not done for reward. I want to make that very clear. Actually I did receive payment, but the amount was so small as to be immaterial. Mr. Duffes did me no disservice—as he feared he could—when he told the Court that nationality meant nothing to me, and that I was neither an unrepentant offender against the laws of the country nor a whining penitent.

My eyes were open all through, and I simply took what was coming to me.

Well, I left Hamburg in February, 1937. It may be thought that I did so for the express purpose of spying. I did not. My daughter, Marga, was really the cause.

As I stated last Sunday, she wanted to take up a stage career, but was prevented because the Nazi authorities thought she might have Jewish blood in her veins. She was unable to prove

Mrs. Jordan before her hairdresser's shop in Dundee where she was arrested.

The photo and signature on Mrs. Jordan's German identity card.

would stay on in her own home in Hamburg for a little, and would probably follow me later.

I had a rough idea of the kind of information that was needed by Germany, and this I tried to put into the sketch. The place was an important one, and I did my best to make my sketch good.

Later, in Court, I learned that I had been successful. The Solicitor-General told the Judge that my work would be of very great value to the pilot of an enemy bombing 'plane which was seeking that particular objective.

Well, that was that, and I breathed a sigh of relief when I finally

On those occasions I stayed with Mrs. Annie Hess, of 23 Stirling Street,

round. I walked round the barracks, quite slowly, and reached the back.

There I saw an open gate and looked through. For a moment or two I stood undecided. Then I boldly entered. After all, I was just a visitor.

After this, I went back to Southampton to get my train for Bremen. Having to change at Bath, and having two hours to wait for a connection, I spent the time looking at business premises, but found none suitable.

All this took place about the middle of June. I returned to Perth with photographs of Southampton and its docks in my possession. I was perfectly genuine in my search for a business. I needed one to live.

Back in Scotland, I carried on my work for Germany. Part of it was to receive letters from U.S.A. and forward them to Germany. I had no idea who wrote the letters or the nature of their contents.

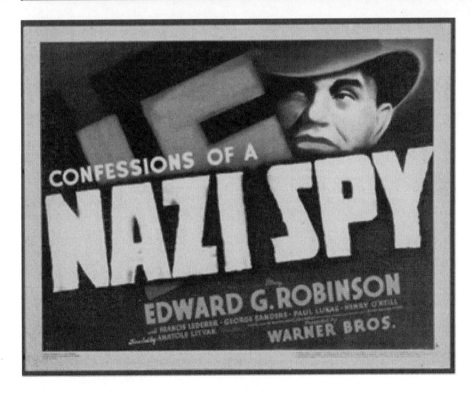

Postie delivering mail to a Mrs McLaughlin (aka Jessie Jordan, Confessions of a Nazi Spy).

Breadalbane Terrace

9 Wing Commander Forgrave Marshall Smith

A resident of Dunning for many years, Wing Commander Forgrave Marshall Smith, D.F.C., RAF No. 37613, Hiram (as he was known) was born in Victoria, Alberta, Canada on 17August 1913, to Thomas and Margaret (nee Marshall), both born in Canada. Thomas and Margaret were married in 1904 in Montreal. Thomas died on 31 October 1967 aged 90; his wife having passed away in April 1965, aged 91. Both had been living in Edmonton, Canada at the time of their deaths. Hiram was their only child and was educated at Oliver & Westmount High School and Victoria High School

Hiram joined a local militia unit when he turned 20 and spent three years learning all about the Canadian Army. He was, however at the same time pursuing his private pilot's licence at the North Alberta Aero Club. In 1935, Hiram was documented as a civil servant, living with his parents and sister at 11033, 86th Avenue, Edmonton, Alberta.

In late 1935, Hiram decided that a life in aviation was what he wanted. He made his way to England and was accepted into the Royal Air Force (RAF). On 11 March 1936, Hiram was granted a short service commission as an acting pilot officer on probation, with effect from – and with seniority of – 2 March 1936. He reported to RAF No. 3 Flying Training School at RAF Grantham, Lincolnshire on 14 March 1936

A little more than a year later the newly promoted pilot officer joined RAF No. 1 (Fighter) Squadron at RAF Tangmere, Sussex flying Hawker Fury biplanes. Smith's stay with No. 1 Squadron was short-lived as a rapidly expanding RAF used 'B' Flight from the squadron on 22 February 1937 to form the nucleus of a new unit.

RAF No. 72 (Fighter) Squadron was based at RAF Church Fenton, North Yorkshire and, in late March, Smith joined the squadron where he honed his skills on Gloucester Gladiator biplane aircraft. In April 1939, No. 72 Squadron was re-equipped with brand-new Supermarine Spitfire Mk. 1 aircraft. Smith was one of the first Canadians to fly this potent fighter.

During the opening months of the war, the squadron flew convoy and defensive patrols, only occasionally coming to grips with the enemy. In the northern part of England and into Scotland the weather was often atrocious. At the end of a long patrol over the water, returning pilots were often greeted with rain and fog. More than once Smith just managed to make a 'blind' landing or was forced to divert to another airfield with mere 'fumes' remaining in his gas tank. It must have seemed to the aviators of RAF 72 Squadron that meeting the Luftwaffe in combat was a safer proposition then dealing with English and Scottish weather.

Flight Lieutenant F. M. 'Hiram' Smith claimed the first victory for RAF 72 Squadron on 4 September 1939. Taking off from RAF Church Fenton at 12.05 hrs, he was to intercept a barrage balloon that had broken away from its moorings. Forty minutes later he brought down the balloon down near Pateley Bridge about 40 miles northwest. Flying Officer's Sheen and Eldson of RAF 72 Squadron whilst patrolling the East Coast of England on 21 October 1939 encountered fourteen Heinkel, He 115, 3-seat seaplane torpedo bombers attacking a convoy and shot down two of them.

RAF 72 Squadron was temporarily stationed at many other airfields before the Battle of Britain began, sometimes just for days, or a week or two. These temporary stays were used to rest and re-group. RAF Leconfield in the East Riding of Yorkshire was taken over in October 1939 by RAF Fighter Command and the Spitfires of RAF 72 Squadron were the first squadron to arrive, though not for long: they were sent up to RAF Drem in East Lothian that same month. In January 1940, they were recalled to RAF Leconfield and then assigned to RAF Church Fenton where they remained until March 1940.

On 1 June 1940, RAF 72 Squadron were ordered south and saw five days of flying over the beaches at Dunkirk, Operation Dynamo covering the evacuation of the British Expeditionary Force and other allied troops. On one occasion Hiram Smith's Spitfire had a failure of the engine coolant pump. He landed with the cockpit filled with, as he noted in his log "a cloud of Glycol steam". Another note is his log for this time states that he returned to RAF Shoreham (Brighton) "by the Grace of God, with 2½ Gallons left".

Despite fog so thick that they could not see the top of the hangars, on 4 June 1940 they were demanded to take-off 'at any cost' from RAF Gravesend. Returning to the airfield was hair-raising, a section landed at RAF Manston, an attempt narrowly missing at church steeple. Two Spitfires landed in a farmer's field. Hiram Smith landed 60 miles further west at RAF Shoreham near Sevenoaks with only fumes left in his petrol tank.

Flight Lieutenant Smith (by now a section leader) dealt with increasing German attention throughout June and July as the Luftwaffe (night-time) attacked their airfield at RAF Acklington on a regular basis. Several aircraft were dispersed to satellite fields to avoid being bombed. At RAF Woolsington pilots had to sleep on chairs in the Flying Club longue as no other accommodation was available.

Flight Lieutenant Ronald Alexander Thomson from New Zealand on 26 June 1940 shot down A Junkers Ju 88 which had been caught in searchlights, one of the few night victories gained in a Spitfire. Thomson began his training on 16 November 1936 at No. 11 E&RFTS (Elementary & Reserve Flying Training School), RAF Perth (Scone).

Hiram Smith on 29 June 1940 (with two other members of the section) was credited with one-third of an enemy aircraft destroyed. Hiram Smith, leading three Spitfires of Yellow Section, scrambled from RAF Arklington and intercepted a solitary Dornier Do 17 which had been spotted about 10 miles from Holy Island. After flying for 40 minutes, they overtook the Dornier at 23,000 feet and Smith flashed a recognition signal at it. They received no response; the aircraft was then recognized as a 'Flying Pencil'.

Hiram circled the Dornier and closed to point-blank range from astern. He raked the Dornier with his machine guns. He was hit by defensive fire from the bomber and broke off his attack. Two other members of the section took their turn and then Hiram attacked from the enemy's port quarter from about 50 yards away. The Dornier went into a spiralling dive and crashed into the sea.

Back at RAF Arklington it was discovered that an armour piercing bullet had just missed his Glycol tank, smashed into the engine rocker box, and had bounced along the rocker arms without breaking anything. Hiram was given the bullet as a souvenir by the aircraft mechanics. It was later learned that the Dornier was on a reconnaissance mission and was carrying a senior member of the German Meteorological Service.

Hiram was in the thick of things again on 15 August 1940 when RAF 72 Squadron was part of an RAF response to numerous German attacks throughout the day. Heinkel He 115's made a feint attack towards Edinburgh, hoping to draw the defending RAF fighters north. German reports were that the RAF had suffered heavy losses in the south and the north would only be lightly defended. In fact, there were six Spitfire squadrons, a squadron of Boulton Paul Defiant's and a squadron of Bristol Blenheim's waiting for them. Most of the pilots in these squadrons were experienced, having fought in the previous two months over France and Dunkirk. They were now well rested and re-equipped. The Germans were also unaware that a 28-ship convoy was due to sail at noon from Hull, and all radars stations had been warned to be particularly alert. Anstruther Radar was first to report two formations of enemy aircraft approaching, one of which turned back about 40 miles from the coast of Scotland.

At eight minutes past noon radar stations began to plot a formation of 20+ enemy aircraft opposite the Firth of Forth. An hour later, the estimates rose to 30, in three sections, heading south-west towards Tynemouth. At Watnall, Fighter Command for the Midlands, they noted the approach of 13 Group's first daylight raid. Scrambled in the afternoon at 12.15pm, RAF 72 Squadron and two other squadrons encountered more than one hundred Luftwaffe aircraft of Luftflotte 5 from bases in Denmark and Norway.

With an hour's warning the fighter controller was able to put squadrons in an excellent position to attack. RAF 72 Squadron Spitfires were placed in the path of the enemy off the Farne Islands, about 25 miles to the north. They climbed to 18,00 feet and were the first to attack. It came as a bit of a shock to them when the 30 enemy aircraft materialised, 65 Heinkel He 111's and 34 Messerschmitt Bf 110's. Squadron Leader E. Graham led RAF 72 Squadron straight into the attack from the flank with one section attacking the Bf 110 fighters and the rest the He 111 bombers. Hiram Smith was leading four aircraft of Red Section. The Me 110s formed defensive circles whilst the He 111s split up. Some jettisoned their bombs in the sea and headed back to Norway.

A Messerschmitt Bf 110 streaked past Hiram, he saw a circle of six close and locked onto the last one. He emptied his guns into it noticing some effect. Aircraft were criss-crossing the sky in all directions with plumes of smoke marking the departure of several enemy aircraft. The fight lasted just five minutes. The surviving German aircraft were set upon again five minutes later by Hawker Hurricanes of RAF 605 Squadron followed ten minutes later by Hurricanes of RAF 79 Squadron. Pressing on the surviving Germans met Spitfires of RAF 41 Squadron. When they arrived at the coast, they found unbroken cloud from 10,000 feet to the ground making it impossible to bomb any of their intended targets. They jettisoned their bombs and headed for home, still harassed by newly refuelled and re-ammunitioned RAF fighters. Hiram recalled the event as:

"Turning in behind a formation of bombers, I opened fire at one hitting its starboard engine, which started to smoke and large pieces flew off the main plane. I swung quickly behind another bomber firing a short burst into its port engine. I then transferred the attack to the third Heinkel, closing to point-blank range and I could see the incendiary bullets flash as they ricocheted on contact. I was close astern when the aircraft blew up with a tremendous explosion and disintegrated in a ball of fire, which I narrowly avoided flying into."

The Luftwaffe lost eight bombers and seven fighters with several more damaged, all without any RAF losses. Further south, another unescorted raid of 50 Junkers Ju 88s from Aalborg in Denmark resulted in more losses for the Luftwaffe. In all, the northern attacks resulted in the loss of 16 bombers out of a serviceable Luftflotte 5 force of 123, and additionally seven fighters out of a force of 34 that were available. Luftwaffe reports indicated that 20% of the aircraft sent had not returned.

When the Battle of Britain started, RAF 72 Squadron was based at RAF Acklington, Northumberland (6 June 1940 to 31 August 1940), but urgently they were transferred on 31 August 1940 to the frontline at RAF Biggin Hill. Biggin Hill suffered severe damage on 30 August 1940. At 1.30 pm successive waves of German bombers started coming in over southern Kent; the third and largest raid began around 4 pm. One of the last remaining hangers was destroyed and most telephone, gas, electricity, and water supplies were cut.

The following afternoon, RAF Biggin Hill was attacked again by high altitude bombers – the damage had meant that two of the three squadrons based there had to be put under the control of nearby control sector stations. The temporary telephone lines installed after the previous days raid at Biggin Hill were destroyed. RAF 72 Squadron operated from the following day, (1 September 1940 to 12 September 1940) out of RAF Croydon.

It was from this airfield on 31 August that Smith's part in the Battle of Britain came to an abrupt halt. During the last two weeks of August 1940, the life expectancy of RAF frontline fighter pilots has dropped to just two weeks. After little more than three hours after arriving at their new home, squadron members were scrambled to engage German raiders. Somehow, Hiram Smith and the three other pilots of his section became separated from the rest of the squadron and found themselves alone in the sky, they had climbed to 20,000 feet over the port town of Rye. More than 100 enemy aircraft were a few thousand feet below them. The four airmen did not hesitate, and dived into them, each man for himself. Smith was immediately challenged by a Messerschmitt Bf 109 making a head-on pass, cannons and machine guns blazing. His first thought was "missed me", but then a 20mm cannon shell exploded with a bang near the left earphone of his flying helmet, fragments of steel penetrated his head, neck, shoulders, and arm. More shells smashed into his Spitfire sending it plunging vertically. Smith's Spitfire was mortally damaged.

With his aircraft spiralling down out of control, the dazed and bloody Canadian, but still conscious, he jettisoned the cockpit canopy and attempted to climb out of the aircraft. The slipstream pinned Smith to the rear of the cockpit, hanging half in and half out of the Spitfire. Later, Smith recalled:

'Every effort having been made to no avail and having gone through the full range of emotions – embracing emergency, frustration, consternation, fear, panic, and supplication, it was clear to me that owing to the speed at which I was approaching the ground, it could only be a matter of moments before I hit it. I then became completely relaxed and resigned to imminent extinction.'

Then suddenly, unexpectedly and for no reason, he found himself clear of the aircraft. Hurriedly pulling the ripcord of his parachute he drifted down to a hard but satisfying landing. In his weakened state, he could not grab the lines of his parachute to collapse it. He was dragged by a strong wind across a field.

After convincing a member of the Home Guard pointing the barrel of a .303 rifle at him, that he was indeed an 'English' airman and not eligible for shooting, he was taken to No. 7 Casualty Clearing Station. Smith survived his extensive injuries, the pieces of steel, according to the surgeon had missed "all the important pipes and things".

Amongst his fellow patients in the RAF hospital at Halton was an old friend, Flight Lieutenant Eric James Brindley 'Nick' Nicolson, VC, DFC. Nicholson was a former member of RAF 72 Squadron; he was awarded the Victoria Cross on 16 August 1940 whilst flying a Hawker Hurricane. He was fired upon by a Messerschmitt Bf 110 injuring him in one foot and the eye. As he struggled to leave his blazing Hurricane, he saw another Messerschmitt. He got back in and continued firing until he saw it dive away to destruction. Then he bailed out and upon landing was fired upon by the Home Guard who ignored his cry of being an RAF pilot. When the pair of them were transferred to the Palace Hotel, Torquay, Flight Lieutenant E. J. B. Nicolson, VC, promptly wrote Hiram out a cheque for £1 in payment for a bet they had taken earlier in the war. The bet was for the first man to be credited with a confirmed kill. Hiram takes up the story:

" We met at the R.A.F. Hospital, Halton, about the end of December 1940. I had sustained 109 cannon shell injuries to my head and neck, and Nick had severe burns to his face and hands. At that time treatment for burns involved liberal coatings of gentian violet, which, added to their injuries, resulted in burns patients not being a pleasant sight … Sometime later I met Nick again at Torquay. Once again, we had been to town at lunch time and, upon returning to the Palace Hotel and entering the front door, Nick was called over to the desk in the hall. I sat down on a settee at the opposite side of the room. A few moments later, a completely shattered Nicolson collapsed beside me and thrust a piece of paper into my

hand. It was a telegram and the message started off 'His Majesty King George VI …', and I thought it must be a joke, but reading on it promulgated 'the award of the Victoria Cross to Flight Lieutenant J. B. Nicolson.' As I finished reading the message, Nick turned to me and said, "Now I have to go and earn it."

After three months in hospital, Smith returned to RAF 72 Squadron. Hiram was promoted to Squadron Leader and posted to command RAF 603 (City of Edinburgh) Squadron at RAF Turnhouse on 1 April 1941. On 16 May 1941 Hiram and his squadron moved to RAF Hornchurch, back into the front line of the battle. Conditions had changed, the RAF were now taking the fight to the Germans with fighter sweeps and bomber escorts over enemy held territory.

Hiram wrote in his logbook, *"on almost every occasion, the formations of Messerschmitt Bf 109's were waiting high in the sun, often well above the RAF raiding aircraft: and they dived down at will on them when they were in a favourable position. They used dive and climb tactics, almost dog-fighting at will with their Bf 109 f's which were slightly superior to the Spitfire V used by No. 603 Squadron, and most other units on the Channel Front in the summer of 1941"*.

Hiram's first success with No. 603 Squadron came on 12 June 1941 when he shot down a Messerschmitt Bf 109 from a range of about 40 yards whilst it was attacking another Spitfire. Two days later, 14 June 1941 he thought he had just damaged another Bf 109 between Dunkirk and Dover in the English Channel. He did not claim this one as he did not see it crash, however other pilots confirmed that the aircraft attacked by Hiram plunged into the sea.

Hiram Smith was rested after two operational tours, 86 sorties and flying time close to 1,000 hours. He left the squadron on 24 July 1941 and on 14 August went to 52 OTU (Operational Training Unit) as Chief Flying Instructor. It was form at RAF Debden and moved to RAF Ashton Down on 31 August 1941.

Smith formed and then briefly commanded RAF 175 Squadron at RAF Warmwell, Dorset, from 3 March 1942, flying Hawker Hurricane IIB aircraft. Hiram then flew with RAF 145 Squadron flying Spitfire Vb's out of RAF Helwan in Egypt and them RAF Gambut in Libya. The Spitfire's key role was to provide high-altitude cover against Messerschmitt Bf 109's and Italian Macci C.202 Foglore (Italian "thunderbolt").

Promoted to Wing Commander, he was posted to India as Chief Flying Instructor at Risalpur. After a course at the Middle East RAF Staff College, Haifa, Palestine, he returned to India and became Wing Commander Operations at Air HQ, New Delhi. Smith returned to the UK for a course at the Fighter Leaders' School and again returned to India, this time to command RAF 902 Wing.

In March 1942, he formed RAF No. 175 Squadron and in August 1942 he went to India where he became Chief Flying Instructor at 151 OTU, Risalpur. In 1944, he attended RAF Staff College at Haifa, Palestine, returning to India in June to become Wing Commander Operations at Air HQ, New Delhi.

He returned briefly to the UK to attend the Fighter Leaders' School and then back to India as Wing Commander, Flying, 902 Wing. He was Joint Assault Commander for the invasion of Ramree Island, on the Arakan coast, Burma. The Battle of Ramree Island (Operation Matador) took place from 14 January 1945 to 22 February 1945. In May 1945, Smith was detached for the invasion of Rangoon, with the task of establishing an airfield. Hiram Smith remained with 902 Wing until the end of the war, following which he led RAF 11 and RAF 75 squadrons off the deck of HMS Trumpeter in the planned but never fully executed Operation Zipper, designed to recapture Singapore. At the end of the war in the Pacific, the Japanese garrison in Penang surrendered (2 September 1945) – the formal Japanese surrender was held in Singapore on 12 September 1945. A Commonwealth force reached Kuala Lumpur on the same day.

During this period, Hiram rose to the rank of wing commander and was awarded a Distinguished Flying Cross, gazetted 30 October 1945. Public Records Office Air 2/9287 has original recommendation by G/C G.P. Marvin dated 27 July 1945 when he was credited with 346 hours operational flying time and was Wing Commander (Flying) of No.902 Wing, No.224 Group:

Wing Commander Smith is in his fourth operational tour and has carried out 280 operational sorties involving 346 hours flying.

This officer's first and second tours were carried out during the Battle of Britain and consisted of interception, convoy patrols, day and night air cover over Dunkirk and sweeps over France and Belgium during which time he carried out 236 operational sorties involving 300 hours flying. During the Battle of Britain, he was wounded in the head by a cannon shell. His third tour was carried out in the Middle East and consisted of bomber escorts and fighter sweeps over Alamein involving 16 sorties totalling 17 hours flying. This tour was terminated on his posting to India.

During the above operational tours, he has destroyed three Ju.88s, one Do.17, one Me.109 and damaged one Me.110 and three Me.109s.

Wing Commander Smith is now in his fourth operational tour and has carried out 28 operational sorties involving 30 hours flying in the Burma theatre of operations. He has taken part in escort to bombers, bombing and ground strafing Japanese positions and sampans over the worst type of country to be found in any theatre of operations. His record shows that he has been almost continuously on operational flying throughout the present hostilities.

As Wing Commander Sweep Leader during his present tour, he has displayed exceptional keenness and has at all times set a very high example to the pilots of the squadrons in the wing.

To this, the Air Officer Commanding, No.224 Group, adds on 4 August 1945:

During his appointment as Wing Commander Flying in the Burma campaign Wing Commander Smith has displayed a fine sense of leadership and his courage and devotion to duty have been largely responsible for the offensive spirit of this wing. This and his previous operational record make him worthy of the award of the Distinguished Flying Cross for which he is strongly recommended.

Wing Commander Forgrave Marshall Smith took part in 280 operational sorties during the war. Hiram retired from the RAF on 13 October 1957 as a wing commander and went to work for British Petroleum as a departmental personnel manager. He was recorded, along with his wife June, on the 1958 and 1959 electoral rolls, as both living at Meadow Croft, Tilthams Corner, Godalming, Guilford, Surrey. (The 1955 and 1956 rolls recorded June at this address, but not Hiram). On the 1960 and 1961 electoral rolls, both Hiram and June were listed as living at Byways, Ridgley Road, Farnham, Surrey, England.

Following his retirement from B.P., and at the time of his death, Hiram and his wife June, resided at Glebe House, Dunning. Hiram is reported to have liked fishing for salmon in the River Earn and his wife June, painting landscapes of the surrounding area. Hiram died of natural causes on 9August 1994, at Hillside Hospital, Perth, Scotland, shortly after his 81st birthday. His death was reported in The Courier and Perthshire Advertiser on 12 August 1994. He was survived by his wife June, two sons (Ian and David) and two daughters (Fiona and Katherine).

Hiram's WW2 1940 to 1941 known tally:

29 June 1940, Dornier Do17 (1/2 claim),

(Spitfire Mk. 1 P9438, 100m East of Isle of May Island, Firth of Forth, RAF 72 Squadron)

15 August 1940, Heinkel He 111 (2 destroyed)

15 August 1940, Heinkel He 111 (probable)

15 August 1940, Messerschmitt Bf 110 (damaged)

(Spitfire Mk. 1 P9438, 300m East of Farne Islands, off Bamburgh, Northumberland, RAF 72 Squadron)

12 June 1941, Messerschmitt Bf 109 (destroyed)

(Spitfire Mk. Va, W3130, 10 miles of Ostend, Belgium, RAF 603 Squadron)

14 June 1941, Messerschmitt Bf 109 (destroyed),

(Spitfire Mk. Va, W3130, between Dunkirk/Dover (10 miles west of Calais), RAF 603 Squadron)

Sources include various websites and books:

The Narrow Margins by Derek Wood and Derek Dempster, 1961

Swift to Battle – No. 72 Fighter Squadron RAF in Action, Tom Docherty, 2009

Canadian Wing Commanders, George Brown and Michael Lavigne, 1984

Notes:

Accounts of aircraft shot down by Hiram on 15 August 1940 have been recorded as 2 x Junker Ju 88 with 1 x Ju 88 probable. His D.F.C. recommendation tally states 5 shot down including Ju 88's, the northern raid he encountered was Bf 110 and Bf 111 aircraft. Junkers Ju 88's from Denmark did attack further south and were met by RAF 73 and RAF 616 Squadrons off Flamborough Head.

Hillside Hospital at Barnhill, Perth closed on 31 December 1997. Glebe House, Dunning, was the former manse of St. Serf's Church.

The attack by the Luftwaffe of 31 August 1940 was Fighter Command's heaviest day of losses. Thirty-nine RAF fighters were shot down with 14 pilots killed. The Luftwaffe lost 41 aircraft in the whole 24-hour period. It was advised at 6.35 pm that all telephone lines to Biggin Hill Fighter Control sector were dead and urgently required was the frequency and call signs of RAF 72 and RAF 79 squadrons. A despatch rider had to be sent to fetch the information. A fourth attack was delivered at 5.30 pm by Junkers Ju 88s and Messerschmitt Bf 110s which further cratered runways, mainly at RAF Hornchurch. RAF Hornchurch and RAF Biggin Hill were, nonetheless, serviceable the next morning.

RAF 72 Squadron nickname, "Basutoland", is derived from the fact that during both world wars, the Basutoland Protectorate, now Lesotho, donated aircraft to RAF, which were assigned to No. 72 Squadron

RAF 54 Squadron was caught in the act of taking off on 31 August 1940. Two sections had got airborne, but the last was blown into the air by explosions. All three pilots emerged shaken and injured but were back on operations the next morning. Thirty Dornier Do 17s dropped about 100 bombs on the airfield; four were later shot down.

The Messerschmitt Bf 110, often known unofficially as the Me 110, was a twin-engine Zerstörer, fighter-bomber.

Flight Lieutenant Ronald Alexander Thomson on 1 September 1940 was shot down in Supermarine Spitfire P9448 by Messerschmitt Bf 109's. Wounded in the chest, lungs, stomach, hands and one leg by shell splinters and with a dead engine he manged a belly landing outside Leeds Castle. He re-joined RAF 72 Squadron at Biggin Hill on 11 October 1940.

Luftflotte 5 at the time of the northern raids was under the command of Generaloberst Hans-Jürgen Stumpff, (10 May 1940 – 27 November 1943). Stumpff served as the representative of the Luftwaffe at the signing of the unconditional surrender of Germany. He was released from captivity in 1947 and died in 1968.

Although lightly armed and with several other design flaws, during mid-1942, in North Africa, the underrated Macci C.202 Folgore achieved a ratio kill/loss better than that of the Messerschmitt Bf 109.

Supermarine Spitfire Mk. 1 K9942 which was flown by Hiram Smith and Flying Officer J. B. Nicholson VC, was restored and is in the collection of the RAF Museum, (hangar 3) at RAF Cosford, north-west of Birmingham.

As a wing commander, E. J. B Nicolson, VC, DFC was killed on 2 May 1945 when a RAF B-24 Liberator from No. 355 Squadron, in which he was flying as an observer, caught fire, and crashed into the Bay of Bengal. His body was not recovered. He is commemorated on the Singapore Memorial. Hiram remained good friends with Nick Nicholson until his death, back in 1940 he became godfather to his son, James.

Research by Ken Bruce and Sue Gibson.

Forgrave Marshall 'Hiram' Smith

THE BASUTOLAND SQUADRON [No.72] (CH 18999) Original wartime caption: For story see CH.18995A Pilots of the Basutoland Squadron at dispersal. Copyright: © IWM. Original Source: http://www.iwm.org.uk/collections/item/object/205441874

THE BASUTOLAND SQUADRON [No.72] (CH 19025) Original wartime caption: For story see CH.18995A Pilots of the Basutoland Squadron. Copyright: ©IWM.Original Source: http://www.iwm.org.uk/collections/item/object/205441895

THE BASUTOLAND SQUADRON [No.72] (CH 18995A) Original wartime caption: The Basutoland Fighter Squadron of the Royal Air Force was one of the earliest Spitfire squadrons in action in the Battle of Britain. The squadron was reformed after the last war in February 1937 and has already five DFCs and two DFMs to its credit in this war. Squadron records show that its pilots have destroyed 83 enemy aircraft and 29 probables with 37 damaged. A line ... Copyright: © IWM. Original Source: http://www.iwm.org.uk/collections/item/object/205441871

RAF FIGHTER COMMAND 1940 (HU 104498) Ground staff re-arm a Spitfire Mk I at Biggin Hill, September 1940. Copyright: © IWM. Original Source: http://www.iwm.org.uk/collections/item/object/205230034

Spitfire IIA 72 Sqn RAF in April 1941 -A Royal Air Force Supermarine Spitfire Mark IIA (s/n P7895, "RN-N") of No. 72 Squadron, RAF based at Acklington, Northumberland (UK), in flight over the coast, piloted by Flight Lieutenant R. Deacon Elliot.

10 Robert and James Stirling

Just over two centuries ago, Reverend Dr Robert Stirling DD (25 October 1790 - 6 June 1878), who was born at Cloag Farm, Methven, invented a simple and elegant engine that is today providing the world with an efficient solar-energy capture device, the ability to 'effectively' sink the pride of the US Navy and is helping to save millions of lives through its use in ultra-low temperature vaccine storing freezers. Stirling is immortalised as one of the most brilliant engineers of all time, but that was not his main occupation, he was, in fact, a minister in the Church of Scotland.

Gadget shops across the world sell models of his engines. A difference in heat is all that is required to power simple Stirling Engine models, the heat from a candle tea light, or just the steam coming from a mug of tea is sufficient.

Some fans of his amazing device even travel to Methven to see where he was born and to stay in the Cloag Farm's holiday cottages (www.cloagfarm.co.uk). From the middle of the Main Street, Methven, a turn north opposite the post office, up College Road leads to the farm, which overlooks the village.

Stirling was in 1816, a Church of Scotland Minister of the Second Charge of Laigh Kirk, Kilmarnock; and by 1824, Minister at Galston. In this area, there were hundreds of coal mines. Robert was witness to many instances of the carnage caused by early steam engines propensity to explode. Although, steam engines were vital for coal mine operation - pumping out water from mines - they were extremely dangerous and were responsible for the deaths of hundreds of miners.

Stirling remembered seeing his mother making jam and came up with the idea of making an engine that was safer. When hot jam is placed in a jar, Robert noticed that the cloth cover rose as the heated air at the top expanded. This gave him the inspiration to develop the concept of heating the air in a sealed cylinder from an external source. His invention has been described as a type of external-combustion engine. His hope was that he would eliminate the need to have any combustible source or pressure boiler within coal mines.

The Stirling Engine works by converting energy made by the expansion of a fixed amount of air or other gas within a closed (sealed) system. A difference in temperature of the air at both ends is all it requires to work. When the air is expanded by heat applied at one end, it pushes up a displacer piston in the cylinder, changing the internal volume of the air. When it reaches the top, where it is cooler, compression and de-expansion of the air makes the piston return. The top of the piston is connected via a linkage to transfer the power and drive say a flywheel, a pump or other workshop machinery. Amazingly the source of power can be either hot or cold. By applying cold to the end of the cylinder, with say ice cubes, the engine can be made to run in the opposite direction.

There are also many variations of the Stirling Engine, which are even more complex. The engine has many assets: a lack of a combustion chamber, the lack of internal heat generation and exhaust output, the ability to be driven by a clean external power source, the lack of a need to cool its cylinders as with gasoline engines, and little noise generation. The first practical 2 hp Stirling Engine was used to pump water from a quarry in Ayrshire in 1818.

Not only was Robert Stirling a world-renowned engineer, but his brother James was just as remarkable an engineer. The brothers learned their skills from their father, Michael, who was born on 18 February 1708, at Glassingall, Dunblane. He was a renowned manufacturer and inventor of a rotary threshing machine (1756-8). In addition, their descendants, Patrick, James and Matthew Stirling became legends in the railway industry throughout the world during the 1800s. The railway engine GNR 4-2-2 No. 1 (Stirling Single) by Patrick Stirling is now part of the National Collection at The National Railway Museum, York.

Subsequent development by Robert and his brother James, successfully increased power output of the Stirling Engine, enough, for example, to drive for three years all the machinery at the Dundee Iron Foundry where James worked as an engineer and manager. James Stirling (20 July 1800-1876) was also born at Cloag Farm. The Dundee Iron Foundry assisted by James Stirling built the 146,000-gallon cast-iron cistern dome water tank, engine, pump, and ball and socket pipes, for Perth's Waterworks (established in 1832 at the corner of Marshall Place and Tay Street (today the Fergusson Gallery)). The building was designed, and the work superintended by then Rector of Perth Academy, Dr Adam Anderson.

Extensive operations were carried out at the Dundee Foundry during James Stirling's time: castings for engines, steam boilers, textile and spinning mill machinery, railway equipment and even a steam engine for a steamship that was built by Garland & Horsburgh. This was the 100-ton steam tug, *Industrien*, built for William Brodie, a Scottish merchant based in Göteborg, Sweden. The Dundee Foundry built the third steam engine for the Dundee to Newtyle Railway' *Trotter,* excluding the tender at a cost of £700. It was put into service on 2 March 1834. James was proud that he managed to run the *Trotter* up the Balbeuchly Incline (between Baldragon and Auchterhouse), 1690 yards on a rising of 1 in 25.

James Stirling further developed the second patented Stirling Hot Air Engine (1841) at the Dundee Foundry, the merit of the original idea belonging to his brother Robert. The new concept was to use compressed air in order to get more power out of the engine. The engine also used an economiser (regenerator or respirator) which reused hot air from the exhaust to increase the efficiency of his air engine - an idea which was also the invention of Robert Stirling. It is still used to this day in many industrial processes to save heat and make engines more efficient. This development may be Robert's most important contribution to engineering.

The initial reception given to the eponymous 1816 Robert Stirling Engine was underwhelming and it was subsequently only sporadically developed. Although the engine is still used today where low to medium power is required - driving small ventilators, pumping water on farms, generating electricity, and pumping air for church organs - its demise came when it was superseded by a safer and much more powerful forms of steam engine and internal combustion engines. Stirling Engines were heavy which ruled out there use in transport applications.

Modern developments in metallurgy changed matters. In the 1950s, the Ford Motor Company looked at the possibility of Stirling Engines being used in vehicles. Since 2004, a Stirling engine has been used to generate energy from concentrated solar power. The Eurodish parabolic array in Seville, Spain, focusses the Sun's solar energy by curved mirrors to a Stirling Engine that in turn drives an electric generator. At one time, it was the most efficient means of converting the maximum of solar energy into electricity.

In 2005, the originally diesel-electric powered, Swedish submarine *HSwMS Gotland*, succeeded in getting past a large US Navy battle group of ships totally undetected on multiple occasions. In a war game exercise with the $4.5 billion aircraft carrier *USS Ronald Reagan* and its escort fleet, the *HSwMS Gotland* just popped up from out of nowhere in the middle of the fleet and took multiple pictures of the carrier to prove that they had "effectively" sank it. Despite all the elaborate anti-submarine technology employed by the US fleet, the $100 million, *HSwMS Gotland* totally bamboozled and utterly demoralised those aboard the US ships.

Stirling Engines are used to 'silently' power diesel-electric submarines in use by the military navies of Sweden, India, Singapore, Japan, China, and many other countries. The Swedish (Saab) Kockums-built Stirling Engine Air Independent Propulsion (AIP) system is used to power an electrical generator for up to 20 knots propulsion and/or charging batteries. Stirling Engine powered submarines can run silent underwater for up to two weeks without the need to surface or snorkel, quietly at perhaps only a slow 5-10 knots, long enough however, to sneak right up to an enemy's coastline without being detected. These submarines are regarded as a cheap alternative to expensive nuclear fission powered submarines.

Stirling Engine powered submarines can use the surrounding sea water as a heat sink to increase efficiency. Modern Swedish stealth submarines use GHOST (Genuine HOlistic STealth) technology. They are designed shape-wise to minimise their radar and passive sonar signature. Gotland class submarines are fitted with 27 electromagnets designed to counteract its magnetic signature to Magnetic Anomaly Detectors (MAD). Its hull has sonar-resistant coatings, and the tower is made of radar-absorbent materials. Interior machinery is coated with rubber acoustic-deadening buffers to reduce sonar detectability.

Stirling Engines have been retrofitted to many existing submarines throughout the world. China operates two types of diesel submarines powered by Stirling engines. The latest Stirling Engine powered Chinese submarine prototype has been claimed to generate 320 kilowatts power output to its electrical generators and the Type 032 Qing-class submarine is capable of submerging for 30 days. It is reported to be the world's largest operational diesel submarine, with seven Vertical Launch System cells capable of launching cruise and ballistic missiles. Three Stirling Engines are being used as a power source in the latest Swedish *Blekinge*-class (A26) submarines.

Since October 2015, the **K**ilopower **R**eactor **u**sing **S**tirling **T**echnolog**y** (KRUSTY) system has been considered by NASA as a power source for interstellar travel and long-duration stays on planets. Some private enthusiasts have built Stirling Engine powered cars, boats and a miniature Stirling Engine was prototyped as a computer chip cooler, using the heat from the chips to drive a cooling fan.

Stirling Engines are used in portable refrigerators and in cryogenics. They are helping to save lives during the current pandemic. They are a component that makes the new class of ultra-low temperature freezer s (ULT freezers) reliable, stable, and efficient. ULT freezers are used to store vaccines and medical samples. The Stirling Engine that has been engineered for this use is hermetically sealed, it requires no oil or lubricants and is nearly maintenance free.

A company in Gloucestershire is currently developing a new type of Stirling Engine based heat pump and refrigeration system. It is claimed to improve the efficiency of heat pumps by at least 50 percent and eliminate the need to use gasses which have a high global warming potential. The remarkable Near Isothermal Stirling heat pump uses Fluid Mechanics patented near isothermal compression and expansion technology.

On 3 October 2014, the Reverend Robert Stirling DD was posthumously inducted into the Scottish Engineering Hall of Fame. Robert Stirling's air engine of 1827 is in the Hunterian Museum, University of Glasgow. Stirling also invented several optical and scientific instruments and was awarded an honorary degree by the University of St Andrews in 1840 in recognition of his scholarly and scientific attainments.

Stirling had seven children and a long ministerial career of 63 years. He was known as the Father of the Church of Scotland when he died in Galston on 6 June 1876. A gifted speaker, Stirling was truly beloved by his flock. He is buried in Galston Cemetery where a new gravestone was erected in December 2014 by public subscription and was rededicated in May 2015.

Notes:

The Dundee Foundry also built 3 locomotives (1838 – 1840) for the Arbroath and Forfar railway, the *Victoria*, *Britannia* and the *Caledonia*. At the time, no less than three establishments in Dundee (the only place in Scotland) were making railway locomotives. The engines built in Dundee by James and George Carmichael, the *Earl of Airlie* and the *Lord Whamcliffe* may have been run the first regular scheduled passenger service in Scotland, in September 1833. (Robert Stephenson's locomotive, the 29 mph *Rocket* at the Rainhill Trials was a few years earlier, in 1829 and three years after James Stirling died was the Tay Rail bridge disaster, 28 December 1879 at 19.16pm)

Patrick Stirling (1820-1895), born in Kilmarnock, was the son of the Reverend Robert Stirling. Patrick was Chief Mechanical Engineer of the Great Northern Railway and was well-liked by the railwaymen of the GNR. For his 70th birthday, they erected a fountain in his honour in Doncaster and 3,000 GNR railwaymen braved pouring rain to accompany his funeral procession when he died.

Patrick's brother, James Stirling was also a locomotive engineer, and Patrick's son, Matthew Stirling was the Locomotive Superintendent (and CME) for the Hull & Barnsley Railway. Another son of Patrick played for Doncaster Rovers and was Mayor of Doncaster. Other sons of Robert Stirling, William, born 1822 and Robert, born 1824 were engineers with the Lima to Calao railway in Peru (the oldest in South America). James, the youngest son, born in 1835, was the Locomotive Superintendent with the Glasgow and South-Western Railway Company and later, the South-Eastern Railway, he introduced many improvements to locomotive power. An attempt to shoot James was made on 29 June 1885. George Hopkins had been a footplateman and following an accident was put in charge of a stationery boiler for the forge at Ashford Works. Due to this accident and a subsequent loss of earnings, he blamed the railway company and tried to murder James Stirling.

Robert Stirling

Stirling Engine, Hunterian Museum, Glasgow

GNR 4-2-2 No. 1 (Stirling Single) by Patrick Stirling, part of the National Collection at The National Railway Museum in York.

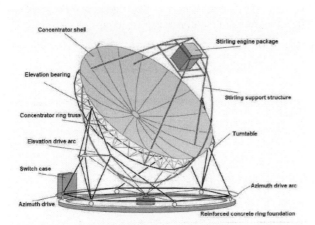

Diagram - Eurodish Parabolic Array, Seville

Stirling Engine – (gadget shop)

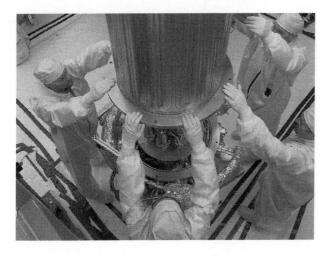

NASA and NNSA engineers lower the wall of the vacuum chamber around the KRUSTY system. The vacuum chamber is later evacuated to simulate the conditions of space when KRUSTY operates. Image NASA

A conceptual drawing of four Kilopower reactors on Mars' surface. Image NASA

11 Victoria Drummond

Victoria Drummond was also a second world war hero who bravely saved the lives of 49 of her ship mates. She sailed as a ship engineer on many dangerous convoys across the Atlantic and Arctic Oceans. Victoria smelled the gunpowder in World War Two before most other woman and men.

It was World War that opened new opportunities for women, and it gave Victoria the chance to pursue a career in engineering. Whilst her parents were shopping in Perth, she went for an interview and was given a week's trial as an apprentice in the Northern Garage, 71 South Street, Perth (where the Salvation Army Citadel is now). She started on 18 October 1916, receiving her first weekly wage of three shillings, of which sixpence was deducted for National Insurance. Her first job was to sweep up the shop floor and put the tools in order on the benches for the day's work. She would wash parts of machinery in a large paraffin bath and scraping of the oil and grease from gear boxes.

Perth at this time of war, was when many long troop trains passed through, many displaying the Red Cross. Victoria took her bicycle with her to Perth and often cycled home the ten miles due to delays caused by additional military trains. In 1914, Suffragettes had been on hunger strike in Perth Prison and were horribly force-fed so that they could carry out their sentences. Perth's Cricket Club Pavilion had been burned down by Suffragettes in 1913 and 3,000 women had marched on the jail in 1914 in support of the incarcerated women. There is no evidence that Victoria was involved, rather, that she was busy her role of doing war work and learning her trade. Her sister Jean went off to do highly dangerous war work as a supervisor in the acid section at an explosive's factory in Gretna. She was one of the famous 'munitionettes' or 'canary girls, which was caused by using poisonous nitric acid in TNT production, it yellowed the hair and skin. Her brother John joined the Grenadier Guards as a cadet.

Victoria took evening classes at the Dundee Technical College and special correspondence instruction in Maths and Engineering subjects. Moving on from the Northern Garage after two years, her father got her an introduction to the Caledon Shipbuilding & Engineering Company. At its works at Lilybank, Dundee, she started as a pattern maker for metal casting, the only woman in a company of 3,000 men. In 1919 she was promoted to the finishing shop, joined the Woman's Engineering Society, and completed her apprenticeship in 1920. She stayed on at Caledon until 1922 as a journeyman.

Accidents in engineering shops were something Victoria had her fair share. From a big lump of molten solder falling on her hand, to being crushed when a 10-ton lorry slipped off its jacks and came down on top of her. Fortunately, she survived that accident, but with a broken collar bone and two broken ribs.

When Victoria completed her apprenticeship as an engineer at Lilybank Foundry in Dundee, in the celebration of the event, she followed the long-established custom of "standing treat" to her 70 odd workmates in the form of a night's entertainment at the King's Theatre Music Hall. Seats were reserved in the grand circle and Victoria sat proudly in the center of her foundry mates.

By 1922, she was tenth Engineer on the 10,000-ton passenger liner *SS Anchises* (Blue Funnel Line). In two years, she voyaged four times to Australia and once to China. Victoria Drummond then left to study and attained a Second Engineer's accreditation in 1926.

In the 1930's there was little demand for Marine Engineers and Victoria found it difficult to find work. In March 1938, Victoria and her sister Francis were visiting Vienna just as German Infantry Divisions marched into the city. From there hotel window, they observed the crowds lining the streets and Adolf Hitler go past in a triumphal parade. Back home Victoria was involved in a car accident and again broke her collarbone. Later in 1938 they were in Holland and Belgium, the atmosphere was very tense, it just days before the second world war was about to begin.

At the start of the Second World War, not being able to get a position on a British ship, she worked as an air raid warden in London. The only solution was to serve on a foreign registered vessel. Victoria signed on as the Second Engineer on the Palestine Maritime Lloyd Ltd. *SS Har Zion.* On 21st March 1940 the convoy they had joined lay off Gravesend. Three ships that had sailed earlier were hit by mines and sunk. In the middle of a minefield, they had to stop to make repairs and a torpedo just missed them by about 15 feet. After dry dock repairs in Antwerp, they returned across the Channel. Victoria witnessed three mines blow up as they passed. Back at Gravesend with the convoy they went through two air raids, with mines exploding in the harbour. A few days later another ship moving anchorage hit a mine, Victoria watched it sink in 2 minutes.

Next, they were off to Lisbon, Gibraltar, Beirut, and Haifa. Victoria broke one of her fingers in her right hand which needed to be put in a splint. From Haifa they went to Port Said, Alexandria and then on to Marseilles. The cargo they collected there was human, the Consul, his staff and the remains of the British Expeditionary Force were loaded and taken to Casablanca. The convoy was attacked by German aircraft on the way home, it returned to London on 20 July 1940. There is mention in some accounts of Victoria's life that she took part in the Dunkirk evacuation. At that time Victoria would have been onboard ship in the Mediterranean.

Three weeks after returning Victoria, at the age of 45 joined the Panamanian registered 3,500-ton *SS Bonita* as Second Engineer at Southampton. On 6 August 1940 the ship set sail for the United States. At Portland they were bombed by German aircraft, Victoria hit her head on an oil box and her watch was smashed. One bomb had missed the ship by only 10 feet, and they were only 20 feet away from having one come down through the engine room skylight. The ship anchored at Fowey in Cornwall until 23 August 1940 when they set off into the Atlantic. As a Panamanian ship with a Hungarian Captain, in effect an enemy alien, they were not thought of as in need of convoy protection.

The next day they saw a dozen or so, St. Malo fishing boats with their sails strung out in a long line. The following day the ships Mate was concerned, the water was too deep for fishing, they were 300 miles out from the nearest land, and he wondered if they were spying on them. He had hardly expressed his concerns when there was a burst of machine-gun firing from an aircraft, it was 8.55am.

Within 2 minutes, Victoria returned to the engine room just as a bomb struck near the ship. She was flung by the shock against the levers of a control panel. Bruised, she struggled to her feet and gave the ship all the speed it could. This was the only hope of survival, to dodge the bombs from the aircraft. Terrific vibrations began shaking the ship, lagging came off the pipes and fell like snow. The ship felt as if it was being lifted and dropped each time the bombs exploded. The noise drained out the sound of the engines and in the confined space of the engine room it was a lot worse. The bombs were big enough to lift the Bonita and could still cause damage by their near misses. The Radio Operator sent the message: BEING ATTACKED, BEING BOMBED AND MACHINE-GUNNED, SEND FIGHTERS QUICK!

Flying debris hit the main water service pipe to the main engine and scalding hot water was gushing out. The speaking tube to the bridge broke off, no instructions could be received, the engine room was on its own. Victoria ordered everyone out of the engine room. There was fuel oil running down her face and she could only see out of one eye. The engine was a hissing burbling inferno, and everything was shaking and banging in an inferno of noise and steam, and she was alone. It was her duty to keep the engines running, the danger was tremendous, but she protected her hands and held back the escaping steam from the damaged joint, her actions maintained the power of the ship.

When the noise of the aircraft warned her that they were about to attack, she eased down the engines, when she heard them circling overhead, she increased steam. The *SS Bonita* had never exceeded 9 knots, but in 10 minutes, Victoria had managed to increase speed to 12.5 knots. With the extra speed the captain used to avoid being hit. Victoria stated later that 25 bombs were dropped, and many machine gun bullets had hit the ship; this suggests that 6 or 7 Luftwaffe long-range Focke-Wulf Fw 200 Condor aircraft took part in the attack, each could carry four kg bombs.

Thanks in no small part to Victoria's actions the *SS Bonita* survived the attack. Victoria was commended for her bravery by Captain Herz, and First Mate Warner as "the most courageous woman I ever saw". The Times newspaper would quote the official report, *"Her conduct was an inspiration to the ship's company and her devotion to duty prevented more serious damage to the vessel."* Victoria's action saved the ship, and she was awarded an MBE and a Lloyds' war medal for bravery.

Once the damage to the engine room had been repaired and without further incident, they reached Norfolk, Virginia in the United States. Victoria's heroism was reported in all the newspapers. Whilst in Norfolk, Victoria learned that her sister's home in Lambeth, London had been bombed. Victoria spoke at various charitable events in Norfolk and enough money was raised to build a green painted Victoria A. Drummond British-American Restaurant in Lambeth, for people who had been bombed out of their homes. With gifts of food, over 350 people a day were fed there. This canteen served hot meals for sixpence a head and remained open for the rest of the war. In April 1941, £400 had also been raised towards the provision of the Victoria A. Drummond Ambulance for the people of Lambeth.

The near sinking of the *SS Bonita* did not deter her, and Victoria Drummond worked on several ships for the duration of the war crossing the Atlantic many times, and on convoys to the Soviet Union. She was on 'Special Ops' duty ferrying stuff back and forth to the beachheads in Normandy on D-Day. Victoria was still to come under fire on more than one occasion and suffered many injuries in the course of her duty, including dislocating her jaw and collarbone twice.

Victoria was encouraged by her father to choose her own career; she chose to be a marine engineer.

Born into a privileged but incredibly supportive background, as a debutante she was presented during her coming-out at Buckingham Palace in February 1913 to King George V and Queen Mary. The respect she earned from her peers and her country made her one of the greatest women of the last century.

By her ground-breaking drive, ambition, grit, and sheer determination, and without any concessions made because of her gender; she became the first Chief woman Marine Engineer. Victoria Drummond was a very highly regarded trailblazer who opened doors for many other women to follow. No woman had done that before at the time, nobody had ever imagined or thought that a woman could.

The war over, Victoria Drummond returned to Scotland. She found employment in the ship building industry and on various cargo ships. The period 1952-57 saw her again as a Second Engineer and finally from 1959 until 1962, she was a Chief Engineer. Thirty-seven attempts to gain accreditation as a Chief Engineer all ended in failure. Undaunted, she finally managed to obtain a Panamanian Chief Engineer's certificate.

Miss Victoria Alexandrina Drummond (1894-1978) was the daughter of Captain Malcolm Drummond and Geraldine Margaret Tyssen-Amherst Drummond of Megginch Castle near Erroll. Victoria had a brother John, and a sisters, Jean, and Francis. Victoria was the granddaughter of first Baron Amherst of Hackney and was named after godmother, Queen Victoria.

Victoria Drummond retired after forty years at sea and died in 1978 aged 84, She is buried where she was born, at Megginch Castle. A plaque at Abertay University in Dundee commemorates Victoria Drummond's achievement as a marine engineer. Victoria was also the first woman engineer of the Institute of Marine Engineers and has the distinction of being the first female chief engineer in the Merchant Navy.

Notes:

There is no evidence of Victoria being given an easier time by her shipmates, in truth she had to fight and work very much harder to prove to everyone her competency as an engineer. Entrenched sexist attitudes within the maritime industry operated against Victoria Drummond throughout her career. What she had to put up with on the way to becoming a Chief Engineer is best summed up by these lines published in the Shields Daily News:

"Women are no substitutes for men in the engine room of a ship at sea," said Mr. C. Booth, district secretary of the Amalgamated Marine Workers Union at Liverpool in January of 1923.

He believed Miss Victoria Drummond will be the last as well as the first woman ship engineer.

"The owners of the Blue Funnel Line allowed Miss Drummond to sail in the SS Anchises to enable her to complete her 18 months at sea and qualify to become a fully certified engineer, and there is not the least chance of their repeating the experiment," said Mr. Booth.

"She is not likely to go to sea again, I should imagine."

How wrong he was, Victoria was to set sail again and yet again over the next forty years.

MISS VICTORIA DRUMMOND, O.B.E.
Miss Drummond, the only woman engineer in the Merchant Navy, is seen leaving Buckingham Palace after receiving the O.B.E.
(See Chapter X)
Photo Planet News

15

12 Lieutenant John Watson McCash

The Royal Flying Corp squadron of a young incredibly brave young pilot from Perth was equipped with the new outstandingly manoeuvrable Sopwith Camel aircraft in October 1917, just in time for the Battle of Cambrai one month later where in a dogfight with the Red Baron's Flying Circus, he was shot down.

Towards the end of the year 1917, the First World War, the war to end all wars, was to see the first large-scale effective use of tanks at the Battle of Cambrai (20 November 1917 – 7 December 1917) in France. Rittmeister Manfred Freiherr von Richthofen, the Red Baron, was just returning to command his flying circus after convalescent leave following a serious head wound that he received on 6 July 1917.

Lieutenant John Watson McCash of The Black Watch, attached to the Royal Flying Corps (RFC), was reported as missing in the Perthshire Advertiser on Wednesday 5 December 1917. He was the 24-year-old son of William F McCash (Grain Merchant, J McCash & Son) and Alice H McCash, Cornhill House, Jeanfield Road, Perth. Lieutenant McCash was the nephew of J B McCash, Solicitor, Perth. The firm of J. McCash & Sons of Dovecotland, Perth have been supplying animal feed since 1746.

John Watson McCash was educated at Clifton Bank School, St Andrews, and later the University of St Andrews. He studied civil engineering and worked for the Caledonian Railway Company in Perth. He enlisted in the Scottish Horse, a Yeomanry regiment of the British Army's, Territorial Army. The Scottish Horse fought as the 13th Battalion of The Black Watch during the First World War. McCash was promoted to corporal and was commissioned in October 1913 into The Black Watch, 6th Battalion, as an officer. He was then attached in April 1917 to the RFC as a pilot serving with No. 3 Squadron of the RFC. At the time of his death was flying from an Advanced Landing Ground (ALG) at Bapaume. In October of 1917, his squadron was equipped with Sopwith Camel aircraft which were just being introduced to the fighting on the Western Front in France.

On 20 November 1917, at dawn, approximately 6.20 am, the British launched an attack at Cambrai (Schlacht von Cambrai) in the département of the Nord, Hauts-de-France region. Six British infantry divisions led by 320 tanks created on the first day a hole in the German defences ten kilometres wide and six kilometres deep. The town of Cambrai was an important supply point for the German Hindenburg Line (Siegfriedstellung) and it's capture along with the nearby Bourlon Ridge would threaten the rear of the German line to the North. The British infantry carried forward the momentum of the attack, they reached a point five kilometres from the *Luftstreitkräfte* (Imperial German Air Service) (Flying Circus) Jasta 11 base at Boistrancourt where they began shelling the airfield, the Jasta retreated to an improvised base at Valenciennes.

On 22 November 1917, the weather prevented flying except at extremely low height, but on 23 November, bitter air combat took place. Just after noon, Jasta 5 Flying Circus aircraft engaged Sopwith Camels over Bourlon Wood. Three Camels got on the tail of Jasta 5's commander, Oberleutnant Richard Flasher, who was saved by the intervention of Vizefeldwebel, (Leutnant der Reserve), Fritz Rumey and Leutnant Otto Könnecke. Both pilots were reported to have shot down one Sopwith Camel each. In fact, only Fritz Rumey received credit for both.

The Sopwith Camels, B5153 & B2369, shot down were piloted by:

Lieutenant Frederick Henry Stephens, 3rd Squadron RFC & Canadian Infantry, age unknown (Canadian)

Lieutenant John Watson McCash, 3rd Squadron RFC & 6th Battalion, Black Watch (Royal Highlanders), age 24

The body of John Watson McCash was not found. He is commemorated at the Arras Flying Services Memorial (Commonwealth Graves Commission) which is in the Faubourg d'Amiens Cemetery, Arras, France. McCash is also remembered on the War memorial in the parish church at Tibbermuir and the book of remembrance at St Andrew's University.

Second Lieutenant W F McCash, a son of Mr and Mrs McCash of Queen Street, Craigie, Perth, educated at Perth Academy and a member of the firm of James McCash & Sons, Grain Merchants, was awarded in early 1917 the Military Cross. Lieutenant McCash was 29 years of age enlisted in the Black Watch at the start of the war. He had been at the front for eight months when he received his commission in The Gordon Highlanders. When he returned to the front he was severely wounded in November 1917. The Gordon Highlanders also took part in the Battle of Cambrai.

Notes:

During the Second World War another member of the McCash family, Pilot Officer James McCash, was killed ferrying a Bristol Blenheim to Tunisia on 18 June 1940. For more details see the madeinperth.org website.

Jagdgeschwader 1 (JG1) had been rushed from Ypres to Cambrai by 23 November 1917, following the launch of the British offensive, and did much to stabilise the air war over the battlefield when the bad weather permitted. Perhaps John McCash's Squadron was unaware of or not expecting to come up against the Flying Circus over Cambrai.

Vizefeldwebel, (Leutnant der Reserve), Fritz Rumey. Rumey was one of the Flying Circus pilots of Jasta 5 which was one of the four squadron wings (Jasta's) in Jagdgeschwader 1 (JG1) under the command since 26 July 1917, of Rittmeister Manfred Freiherr von Richthofen, known as the 'Red Baron', (in German as the 'Der Rote Kampfflieger'). Fritz Rumey was one of the very best aces, if you take away the number of reconnaissance aircraft shot down and look at just the number of combat fighter aircraft shot down, his tally was 45, Richthofen's only 35.

A replica of Rumey's Albatross aircraft was built in 2016 by The Vintage Aviator Ltd in Wellington, New Zealand. They have built several full-scale, 100% accurate reproductions of WW1 German Albatros D.Va fighters. It may have been re-painted since then.

On the side of the aircraft, there is a picture of his demon head motif, this was how his aircraft was re-painted when Richthofen took over command in July 1917 at Boistrancourt airfield (French: Aérodrome de Boistrancourt-Suererie, german: Feldflugplatz Boistrancourt).

Perhaps in my view, the two best aircraft at this time during WW1 were the German Albatros D.Va and on the British side, the Sopwith Camel. You had to be good to fly either, both were extremely deadly in the right hands as fighter aircraft.

Rittmeister Manfred Freiherr von Richthofen was flying in his red Albatross D.V. above Bourlon Wood that day, about an hour later. He forced the pilot of a No. 64 Squadron, Airco D. H. 5 aircraft to make an emergency landing. His next victim was Lieutenant J A V Boddy flying D. H. 5, A9299, his gun had jammed, and he was trying to clear it when Richthofen's red Albatross opened fire on him. A bullet fractured his skull but somehow, he manged to land his aircraft near the northeast corner of the wood, additionally breaking his thighs. Boddy recovered from his injuries, but his flying days were over. No. 64 Squadron lost six D.H. 5's that day. None of the pilots were killed, but two were wounded.

The Royal Flying Corp losses for 23 November 1917 was 14 with 15 enemy aircraft claimed shot down. In the air that day over Cambrai, were several other notable 'Aces', Manfred's brother. Lothar Richtohfen, and Captain James T B McCudden, VC, DSO & Bar, MC & Bar, MM (57 victories). McCudden first served with 3 Squadron RFC as a mechanic and then observer (June 1913 – January 1916) before becoming a pilot. On the ground, Private Archie McMillan of the Argyll and Sutherland Highlanders was one of many thousands killed on the ground, he was a footballer with Glasgow Celtic.

The Royal Flying Corps was established in 1912, just three years after Louis Bleriot had flown across the English Channel. The RFC during 1914 and 1915 the recruits were mainly professional soldiers who had already seen some action in the trenches. By 1916, many of the new recruits were volunteers and those who were technically skilled railwaymen, such as John McCash were much favoured by the RFC.

On 26 July 1917, the Royal Prussian Jagdstaffel 11 squadron of the German air force, commonly known as Jasta 11 became part of Jagdgeschwader 1 (JG1). This was a wing of four Jastas under the newly arrived command of Rittmeister Manfred Freiherr von Richthofen, known as the 'Red Baron', (in German as the 'Der Rote Kampfflieger'). Rittmeister Richthofen had just flown to Boistrancourt airfield, (French: Aérodrome de⬛Boistrancourt-Suererie/German: Feldflugplatz⬛Boistrancourt) 100 miles north-west of Paris to take charge of the newly combined Jasta's operation.

Richthofen was severely wounded in the head on 6 July 1917 and returned to his command on 25 July 1917. JG1 were the first squadrons to receive the new Fokker DR.1 triplane, as famously associated with the Red Baron. The first two were received on 21 August 1917. The German Ace pilot, Werner Voss was perhaps the greatest exponent, scoring ten victories in just 21 days before he died in combat. Rittmeister Richthofen left on convalescence leave on 6 September, returning on 23 October 1917. Richthofen spent time hunting on the estate of the Duke of Saxe-Coburg-Gotha (German: Sachsen-Coburg und Gotha), visiting his family at Schweidnitz and going to Adlershof for more consultations about aircraft design. Adlershof was the headquarters of the German Experimental Institute for Aviation (Deutsche Versuchsanstalt für Luftfahrt – DVL). During Richthofen's time away, several fatal crashes involving the new Fokker DR.1 saw it withdrawn for modifications. They were grounded from 23 October 1917 until early December 1917.

Fritz Rumey was a German 'Ace', credited at the time of his death with 45 victories. He was a holder of the Pour le Mérite (Blue Max) and the Goldenes Militär-Verdienstkreuz (Golden Military Merit Cross). He was only one of five pilots to receive both these awards. There are two accounts of Rumey's death on 27 September 1918, that following a mid-air collision with a Royal Aircraft Factory S.E.5a of 32 Squadron flown by Captain G E B Lawson, his parachute failed to open, and he threw it away. The second account, that during a full throttle pursuit of the S.E.5, it caused the fabric to peel off from his upper wing and this caused his aircraft to fall from the sky and crash. Lawson survived and was awarded a DFC, Lawson later died in a flying accident in 1922. Parachutes were also used in limited numbers by the Germans in the last months of the war. Famously, Flying Circus 'Ace' Ernst Udet used one on 29 June 1918 following a mid-air crash with a French Breguet aircraft.

Leutnant Otto Könnecke survived the war, he died 25 January 1956, age 64. During the Great War he received the Pour le Mérite (Blue Max), the Goldenes Militär-Verdienstkreuz, Knight's Cross with Swords of the Royal House Order of Hohenzollern and the Iron Cross. His tally was 35 victories.

Manfred von Richthofen's death was to come on 21 April 1918 when he was killed following an attack by the Canadian, Captain Arthur "Roy" Brown (23 December 1893 – 9 March 1944) in his Sopwith Camel. Brown died of a heart attack just after posing for a photograph with the WW2 Canadian flying ace, George Frederick "Buzz" Beurling (known as "The Falcon of Malta" and the "Knight of Malta"). Cedric Bassett Popkin (20 June 1890 – 26 January 1968) is considered the likely person to have killed Richthofen. Popkin was an anti-aircraft (AA) machine gunner with the First Australian Imperial Force (AIF).

At the Battle of Cambrai, the German artillery and infantry defences exposed the frailties of the Mark IV tank. By the second day of the battle only half the tanks were still operational. The Sopwith Camel first appeared over the third Battle of Ypres (also known as Passchendaele, 31 July 1917 – 10 November 1917), it lasted over 100 days. In that time, the Allies advanced about 5 miles for the loss of over 250,000 soldiers killed, wounded or missing. The overall average life expectancy during the Great War of a pilot was 92 flying hours. There was nonetheless no shortage of volunteers for aircrew training. The Sopwith Camel with its outstanding manoeuvrability made it deadly in the hands of a good pilot. It dominated the skies over the trenches and became the RFC/RAF's main fighter until the Armistice, on the 11th hour of the 11th day of November 1918.

The 2008 movie, The Red Baron starring Matthias Schweighöfer, Joseph Fiennes, Til Schweiger and Lena Headey is the best to watch. The music is also excellent, with a couple of haunting tracks by Dirk Reichardt and Stefan Hansen that linger in your brain.

13 Inchaffrey Abbey

Between Perth and Crieff there was once a rich and historically important abbey. Nowadays very few know of its existence, far less its history and how the Abbot Maurice played a seminal role in Scotland's war with the English at Bannockburn. All that remains are some walls and an earth mound.

How it met its end was not as many other Abbey's during the Reformation, following John Knox preaching in St John's Kirk in Perth on 11 May 1559. The final demise of Inchaffrey Abbey came much later and in rather a gruesome way.

The land that lies along Strathearn was not as fertile and well drained as it today. The Gask Ridge where the Romans had their wooden forts and look-out towers, were more valuable as a safe defence line than you may have thought. They were never intended to stop an army of rampaging Highlanders who had just travelled down the Sma' Glen. The Romans did not fear the Highlanders, they were quite safe from immediate attack, and would have had plenty of time to call up reinforcements from their main forts and encampments. Down below the Gask Ridge looking towards Glenalmond was wet marshy bogland running almost all the way along Strathearn. No rampaging army, even the best was going to be able to cross over and quickly attack the Romans. They would have needed to find safe paths through the bog to cross the valley, which would have taken quite a while to traverse, except perhaps when it was solidly iced over in the winter.

This marshland area had a burn running through it called the Pow Water (also known as the Pow of Inchaffrey). The Pow water is in two parts, roughly from the Methven Moss it goes west to the River Earn, just above Innerpeffray Library. To the east it goes to the River Almond at Lochty/Almondbank. There was talk at one time of making the west part into a canal in order to service the Abbey.

The Pow water was so important that it was the subject of two parliamentary orders, one Scottish Parliament (pre-union) and another at Westminster. The basic premise was to ensure the landowners in the area maintained and improved the water drainage. Parliamentary charters over the years have resulted in the Pow Water being dug even deeper so that the surrounding area could be drained for farming. Even when this was complete, the water in the Pow could still rise to 7 feet during times of flooding. The water was drained away to the East into the River Earn and to the West into the River Almond at Lochty.

The Abbey itself was built on the Isles of the Masses (Insula Missarum) at Madderty, about halfway between Perth and Crieff. Masses meaning offerings, not a large group of people. The about 1200, this religious site does is in fact predated this by more than a few centuries. The site was originally occupied by "brethren" of the old Celtic Church or the Church of the Culdees. It was run by the brethren of St John of Strathearn, the head of whom was designated in some records as the "Hermit ". The Pow provided well for the monks, including a 'lovely' diet of fresh eels.

The Augustinian Abbey was founded and built at Inchaffray around 1200. It was initially funded by the Earl of Strathearn, (Abercairny, just east of Crieff). Inchaffray comes from the Gaelic, *innis abh reidh* (island of the smooth water). It may have been linked to Iona at one time as well. The abbot was also known as the hermit. Later it came under the Augustinian order. In 1275 it was assessed as the fourth richest Augustinian Abbey in Scotland (behind St Andrews. Holyrood and Scone).

What it is truly famous for is its Abbot, Maurice of Inchaffray, Chaplain to Robert the Bruce. Maurice Abbot was the one who heard Bruce's confession and blessed the Scot's army on the field at the Battle of Bannockburn in 1314. When upon seeing this blessing being given, Edward II thought that the Scots were asking for forgiveness, or it is also supposed that he said in surprise that *"They pray for mercy!"* - *"For mercy, yes,"* one of his attendants replied, *"But from God, not you. These men will conquer or die."*

Bruce was a frequent visitor to these parts, he laid siege to Perth about 4 times. Bruce was defeated at Methven Wood just along the road from the Abbey, he would have known the Abbot well. Bruce had previously lost a battle at nearby Methven, 8 years earlier in June 1306. This was the before the start of Bruce's wandering the Highlands and the guerrilla war campaign (pre-Bannockburn, wife captured, spider story etc) Later after the Battle of Bannockburn, Bruce gave Maurice the Bishopric of Dunblane.

There is seemingly an account for lodgings in Perth when Robert the Bruce visited with his pet lion. The keeper was named John and was paid 20 shillings a year from the customs of Perth, which also paid the rent for the 'domus' of the lion and a new cage in 1331. Bruce died 7 June 1329, records for only two years exist for the lion.

Lastly, the gruesome bit, why is the Abbey a ruin? It was not because of the Reformation (Knox etc.), when all the other Abbeys were destroyed. Inchaffray survived this time of turmoil. Its demise came much later, the story goes that a lady, resident in London, filled with the common fear, went, along with her servants in 1665 to Scotland and took up her residence in Inchaffray Abbey (by this time untenanted). She was expecting to find safety and repose. Scarcely had she arrived at her destination than one of her servants died of the disease.

The local inhabitants around heard that the plague was amongst them, and their terror became extreme. They rose *en masse*, barricaded the doors, and set fire to the building, mercilessly determined to consume every soul within. All perished within the Abbey, save a small dog, which by some means escaped, and ran eastwards, carrying the infection with it.

Notes:

If you go out the old Crieff Road and turn right, down the hill at Madderty. At the bottom the road turns right and then left over a small bridge over the Pow. Opposite is a new house built just outside where the Abbey was. If you look hard, you may just see the ruins of the Abbey wall, only a gable end remains. You can also see ruined walls from the other side (parking is difficult). A road was built through it in the 1800's and a house has been erected in the grounds.

The Abbey seems to be one of the few that survived intact after the Scottish Reformation of 1559/60 which started in Perth at St. John's Kirk. The Abbey was abandoned sometime after.

The Pow Water was first dug by locals on the orders of the cannons from Inchaffray Abbey and later King Robert the Bruce granted royal permissions to expand the work. Abbot Maurice of Inchaffray claimed to have witnessed a miracle whereby the arm bone of Saint Fillan appeared in a previously empty reliquary. Robert the Bruce credited the miracle with providing his subsequent victory on the Bannockburn battlefield. In thanks to Maurice, he granted the abbey permission to extend the Pow. The abbey went into decline after the Scottish Reformation and was gradually abandoned. Despite this the Pow remained in use.

The word Pow comes from the Scot's Language, meaning – *pool of water, a shallow or marshy one, a watery or marshy place.*

The road to Crieff originally went out via the Burghmuir Road and along the Gask ridge, the bog below was the reason. It would pass by Innerpeffray and enter Crieff at the lower end of the town. When Kinkell Bridge was built it in 1793 it opened easier travel between the parishes of Findo Gask and Blackford. The new Crieff roads came along when the land of Strathearn was drained.

The new flood defences needed building at Lochty/Almondbank, as all the flood water from both sides of the West part of Strathearn regularly overloaded the Pow water at Lochty.

14 Sergeant Andrew McKenzie Munn

The situation in Europe in the summer of 1939 was deteriorating and as a prudent measure, Leslie Hore-Belisha, Secretary of State for War, persuaded the cabinet of Neville Chamberlain to introduce a limited form of conscription on 27 April 1939. The Military Training Act being passed the following month. Only single men 20 to 22 years old were liable to be called up, and they were to be known as "militiamen" to distinguish them from the regular army. National conscription had ended in 1920. Each man was to be given six months of training before being allowed to return home on an active reserve status. Andrew McKenzie Munn was called up on 15 July 1939 and posted to join the Seaforth Highlanders at Fort George, northwest of Inverness. War was declared on 1 September 1939.

Andrew McKenzie Munn was a hero twice over, he fought with the BEF in France at the start of the War, he was evacuated, wounded, from Dunkirk and later transferred to the RAF as an Air Gunner on Avro Lancaster bombers. Later as an air gunner on Avro Lancaster W8428 on an operation to bomb the docks at La Spezia in northern Italy, he and all the crew on board were killed.

RAF 103 Squadron allocated 20 aircraft for the attack on La Spezia, consisting in total of 208 Avro Lancaster's and 3 Handley Page Halifax aircraft. Three of RAF 103 Squadrons aircraft immediately returned due to mechanical issues, one aircraft failed to reach the target owing to an unserviceable d/r (distance reading) compass, another ditched in the English Channel and Lancaster W8428 failed to return. Bombing height was between 7,000 and 12,000 feet with Pathfinder aircraft going in first to light up the target with flares.

The goal was to cause maximum damage to the target area. Each aircraft had a bomb load of 5 x 1000 lbs G P, T D (General Purpose, Time Delay), 2 x 90 x 4 lbs (incendiaries) and 2 x 8 x 30 lbs (incendiaries). In addition, all aircraft carried cameras and nickels (leaflets). Take off on 13 April 1943 was at 2019 hours, the route taken was directly south from RAF Elsham Wolds to Selsey Bill, Cabourg (France), Lac du Bourget (France) and on to La Spezia in northern Italy, southeast of Genoa.

There was no cloud cover over the target, the anti-aircraft flax was intense at first but soon died down. A dozen searchlights were in operation and a smoke screen was being used to cover the target area. The Pathfinder Force lit up the target with white flares so that each aircraft could pin-point the target individually and bomb from a lower height than usual. Bombing height was between 7,000 and 12,000 feet. The raid, judging by the fires observed was a great success, but the battleships anchored at the port were not visible due to smoke. The bombing force after their long journey, returned to the UK landing between 0545 hours and 0700 hours. Only one aircraft managed to return to base, the others were diverted for an unknown reason to RAF airfields at Westcott, Tangmere, Wyton, Exeter, and Middle Wallop.

Munn and the crew onboard Avro Lancaster W8428 were posted to the War Casualties Non-Effective Accounts Department, as non-effective missing. Their aircraft most probably crashed following a mid-air collision with RAF 12 Squadron Lancaster ED714, over Saint-Mars-d'Outillé, south of Le Mans in France.

The crew of Avro Lancaster W8428 who died on 14 April 1943:

Flight Lieutenant Edward Claude Lee-Brown RAFVR (125695) pilot, age 20

Pilot Officer James Smart RAFVR (144753) navigator, age 19

Sergeant George Watson Houliston RAFVR (974219) flight engineer, age 31

Flight Sergeant James Joseph O'Brien DFM RAF (551549) wireless operator, age unknown

Sergeant Stanley Moseley RAFVR (1351789) air gunner, age 20

Sergeant Andrew McKenzie Munn RAF (657170) air gunner, age 24

Warrant Officer Class 1 James Willis Toon RCAF (R74721) air observer, age 23

The crew were all interred at Le Mans West Cemetery.

Andrew McKenzie Munn was the son of William L Munn and Helen Munn, Coul Lodge, Auchterarder, Perthshire (late of Barnhill, Perth).

These are the missions they flew prior to being killed:

Edward Lee-Brown and his crew were posted to RAF 103 Squadron at RAF Elsham Wolds from RAF 1656 Heavy Conversion Unit on the 29 December 1942.

Their tour of 16 operations is shown below:

04-Feb-43 – Lorient – Lancaster – W4828 – P/O EC Lee-Brown

18-Feb-43 – Wilhelmshaven – Lancaster – W4828 – F/O EC Lee-Brown

21-Feb-43 – Bremen – Lancaster – W4828 – F/O EC Lee-Brown

25-Feb-43 – Nuremberg – Lancaster – W4828 – P/O EC Lee-Brown

26-Feb-43 – Cologne – Lancaster – W4828 – P/O EC Lee-Brown – Early return – MU gunner became unconscious because of failure of oxygen.

08-Mar-43 – Nuremberg – Lancaster – W4828 – F/O EC Lee-Brown

09-Mar-43 – Munich – Lancaster – ED528 – F/O EC Lee-Brown

11-Mar-43 – Stuttgart – Lancaster – ED612 – F/O EC Lee-Brown

12-Mar-43 – Essen – Lancaster – ED612 – F/O EC Lee-Brown

27-Mar-43 – Berlin – Lancaster – W4828 – F/O EC Lee-Brown

29-Mar-43 – Berlin – Lancaster – W4828 – F/L EC Lee-Brown – Did not take off – Passed take off dead line after runway change.

03-Apr-43 – Essen – Lancaster – W4828 – F/L EC Lee-Brown – Had to evade searchlights in the target area. Bombs fell short as a result.

04-Apr-43 – Kiel – Lancaster – W4828 – F/L EC Lee-Brown

08-Apr-43 – Duisburg – Lancaster – W4828 – F/L EC Lee-Brown

09-Apr-43 – Duisburg – Lancaster – ED612 – F/L EC Lee-Brown

13-Apr-43 – La Spezia – Lancaster – W4828 – F/L EC Lee-Brown – FTR – Crashed near Le Mans, France.

Before joining the RAF, Andrew Munn served with the Seaforth Highlanders and was evacuated from France at Dunkirk.

Andrew McKenzie Munn - Personal Account

The following is a personal account, written by Alexander McKenzie Munn about his experiences with the British Expeditionary Force in France 1939/1940. The original personal notes are held by the Seaforth Highlanders Museum.

(Notes in square brackets for clarification by Ken Bruce)

Advanced into Belgium by way of Tournai [west of Lille] travelling in dark, pretty tough going driving without lights – hide out most of the next day in orchard close to Albert Canal where Battalion dug in to take position (about 190kms). Got my first shot at enemy aircraft out on reconnaissance, fired a couple of magazines on the Bren (better luck next time). A few hours later they came back and made a raid on a convoy coming up. Fifteen of them swooped down from the cloud on the tail of the first, dropping their death dealing pills, very exciting to watch, but hell to be near them when they explode. They all got clear despite machine gun and AA fire. That night we took up flank action with the Battalion. Using our Bren Gun Carriers. About 2 am we had just about enough – Gerrie shelled us out despite heavy fire from our own artillery in the rear. It would have been suicide to stay and so we returned with a few losses. It really was very aggravating as we could see precious little to fire at. We lost two of the Bren Gun Carriers, one broke down, and the other was ditched in the darkness, so we scuttled them.

We then stayed two days on the Franco Belgium border at Hal [Halle]. Discovered a chocolate factory that had been evacuated, Boko chocolate for soldier [much chocolate]. I carried a store in carrier only the heat of the engine and the weather did not help much. The worst sight was the poor people flying (fleeing) from their homes. Old men, women and children al on the trek with just one thing in mind – to get as far away from the fighting area as possible. The roads were packed with them, with their few personal belongings flung over their shoulders. That day I got a beautiful view of a battle between a Messerschmitt and a Spitfire, but sorry to relate the Spitfire bit the dust. The Messerschmitt managed to double round and follow the Spitfire up on the tail and gave it a few bursts with the machine-gun. The British pilot made a jump for it and his parachute, and his machine made a perfect nosedive and hit the ground about 500 yards from me, bursting into flames – You talk about 'Hell's Angel', it never had a look in. Shortly after this, we were called away to the region of Arras as we discovered Gerrie was there. How the hell he managed it I could not tell but it sure was an eye-opener for us.

[The Spitfire was most likely a Hawker Hurricane, Spitfires were not sent to France/Belgium with the BEF. The BEF was pulled back to the line of the River Dyle, to the west of Halle, but the Germans had broken

through to the south at Sedan, France. There was a counterattack at Arras, France, but the BEF, French and Belgian forces north of the Somme retreated to Dunkirk soon after.]

The first night we arrived there after being hindered with refugees on the road all day, we were subject to another air raid in a wood which we rested in for the night. I like the word 'rested'. We did not know what it was to rest. There were quite a few boys cracking up under the strain. No wonder when you see the black buggers [Stuka Ju 87 Dive Bombers], about fifty of them screaming overhead, dropping eggs wherever they pleased despite the barrage put up against them. We shot down a few but they still came on. If I was telling a fishy story, I would say they were a 1,000 strong. The burning question with everyone was, 'Where is the famous RAF?' We were beginning to think there was none. After two days of dodging shells, bombs and bullets from the Gerrie Infantry, we were shifted to Ypres [Belgium], what for? Well you better ask the War Office, but this sure was the hottest spot yet. Gerrie accounted for a few of our trucks, but we brought down two of their birds and took one crew alive. They were quite posh looking chaps with heir black tunics, breeches and leggings. Two of them had a few medals on their chest. There must be a Woolworth's in Germany too. They could speak English to a fair extent, their excuse being they might need it one day. You can take that crack both ways. Some of the boys were for lynching them but the officers said they were more useful the way they were, maybe so, I don't know.

We took up defensive positions that night and we were not there for more than two hours when we contacted Gerrie. After a night of popping at them or should I say any black object that moved, dawn broke and then came fireworks? He started shoving his trench mortar, 100 to the minute or so it seemed like anyway. All you could hear was the whistling over your head and exploding in the close vicinity. It was not so bad when they did whistle overhead, you knew at least you were safe anyway. Between the snipes and flying shrapnel, it was sure no paradise, so we decide to advance. The boys fixed their bayonets and pushed forward, boy did Gerrie retreat? I'll say he did. He could not stand the cold steel. Quite a few tried to give themselves up but the 'Jocks' were so het up they gave them all they had. We advanced alright but the Bat. On our right flank did not so we were in a hotter spot than ever. Between front and side fire, not so healthy I may tell you. The boys began to suffer pretty heavy casualties and it was then a nicely placed shell found my carrier which were hidden in a hollow. I was lucky to be out of it all the time. When I saw it go up, I was not feeling in too happy a position, nor was my crew, the officer and sergeant. The only thing I had on me was my rifle and fifty rounds of ammunition.

At that point, the Bat. Decided to retire back a bit as Gerrie was pressing us, it was then some lucky guy drew a bead on me. By God, it fairly stung, so I dropped into a ditch and lay there for I think about one and a half hours. I could hear one or two Gerrie's shouting to each other in guttural tones, but I just lay there still hoping they would pass by. It must have been a patrol because for the next hour I could hear nothing, so I decide to crawl along the ditch hoping I was making the right way. Somehow or other I managed to come in contact with a party of RA's [Royal Artillery] in a small truck by the side of a deserted farmhouse. They were just ready to make a dash for it across an open piece of country to where one of their guns were, so I got in the truck and lay down hoping for the best. Glad to say we only encountered a few stray shots, none of whom hit us, but they were too close to be healthy.

I then arrived at a dressing station behind our lines and had my leg dressed. From there we were put into Red Cross trucks and transported to the coast. We were thirty hours on the road and we only travelled about 100 miles. What with air raids from Gerrie's and the road blocked with traffic, it was a nightmare of a journey. We arrived at our destination, Dunkirk, everything was in chaos. I shall always remember it; the plane was burning all over and the smell and smoke was terrific. Cars, lorries and everything imaginable was left lying around. I managed to salvage myself a new battle dress and a few pieces of new clothing out of a salvaged RASC [Royal Army Service Corps] truck as my own was in a horrible state what with mud and blood on them.

After a few nerve-racking air raids, we managed to get on a ship. Four of them were lying at the end of the pier. I got into a first-class cabin on the 3rd deck, so feeling quite comfortable, I changed into my new togs and had a wash, the first for four days. I head there was tea ready upstairs, so I managed to limp up for some. While we were up there, the sky seemed to be alive with Nazi planes circling away up above, so we knew we were about to get it hot. Down they came one after the other, whining and roaring like the devil, and dropped some of their heavy bombs despite heavy fire from our ships. 'Oh, where is the RAF? Some of their bombs went wild but our ship 'Crested Eagle', and the next one, were hit direct. I can still feel the blast of that bomb. I thought I could write 'finish' to my career. The next minute we got word to leave the ship, which was all very well, but there, was no pier or gangway left, so we were in a bit of a fix? I do not know how some of the wounded manged, but I slid down a rope on to the broken pier and made for the other boat. My leg was fairly giving me hell all the time. After getting as much as possible on board, we cast off 'toot sweet'. The ship was packed tight with men, but everything was not so bad for a while. About five miles out the vultures returned circling round about us. The ship's crew put up a heavy barrage with AA gun and a couple of Lewis machine guns but the aircraft seemed to be blessed by Lady Luck because though a few of the shells burst very near them, they seemed to live a charmed life. They repeated the same tactics as at the pier, diving at full speed and letting go with two or three bombs at a time sometimes the planes were inly about 500 feet up before they brought them out of the dive and boy did those engines whine! I'll say they did, it was really nerve racking the noise they made.

Well as you understand we could not stand that bombardment, so the ship shook from bow to stern as the bombs contacted. What a hell of a din, the blast of hot air smote me across the face about one a second. After Gerrie did as much damage as possible, he drew off leaving the ship just totally wrecked, but still afloat and very surprisingly the engines were still running. How they made it I do not know. The cry went round the ship for fire extinguishers as the damn thing went up in flames. The noise was terrible, between the noise of the dying men and the cracking of burning wood as the fire was getting really desperate. Some of the men broke into song. I mind they sang 'Loch Lomond' and 'Tipperary' at the top of their voices. It made me think of a picture I once saw of the 'Lusitania' before it went down. Everything just looked the same. The heat and smoke were something terrible by now as the ship had turned back and was making for land, we thought we still had a ghost of a chance of life, at least what was left of us. She grounded about two miles out, but a destroyer could be seen steaming to our aid. There was magazine on board and the captain gave orders to jump for it. We were all pretty glad to get away from the heat and smoke which was suffocating us, so I made a bee-line for the side and like a mug dived off instead of jumping – I forgot at the time I was wearing a lifebelt around my neck. The distance to the water was about 15 feet and the impact as I hit the water nearly broke my neck. It was pretty sore for a day or two. When I stuck the water, I started swimming for the shore which now seemed an awful distance away. Too far for my liking. I noticed the destroyer had arrived and lowered a big flat pontoon boat to pick up the unfortunate ones who could not swim. I also noticed Gerrie still floating around way up in the sky. Surprising to relate I felt quite confident when I started swimming for the shore although after a bit the shore still seemed a long distance off. You make slow progress with the lifebelt and of course the salt water in my wound was giving me jip.

I limped up the beach to the sand dunes in front of me and discovered that we were not the only ones to be marooned. There was quite a large number of British soldiers there. I managed to scrape up dry shirt and underpants and I got an old leather coat from a French soldier. By gum – I needed it as the evening was wearing on and I was shivering like a leak. During the night between 2 and 3 thousand troops turned up on the shore and I discovered this was the first of the crowd that was on the retreat. They were to be loaded on to the ships, which were anchored out from the shore. They had come across the channel under cover of darkness. The troops were loaded on small boats, which held only about 10 men a trip, so you can imagine it was a painful night before we managed to get loaded again. Some of the soldiers got fed up waiting and waded out as far as possible and swam the rest, but this was soon stopped as the ships could not cope with them trying to get on board out of the water. It was dawn before I managed to bag a small pleasure boat, which was being used for loading purposes, and would you believe it – it stuck on a sandbank not far out, talk about luck! After about an hour of rugging and tugging, we managed to free it and we embarked safely on a destroyer, from there I fell asleep from pure exhaustion and was awakened at Dover sometime in the afternoon. I landed on English soil with nothing but a shirt, pullover, underpants and a leather coat, which had seen better days, no boots or stockings just like an African native, dressed up. Such is life!

I managed to get equipped on shore, so I made for the hospital train which I boarded and landed in Sheffield and then life was a bed of roses, good food, nice nurses and of all things a good bed.

Very nice reading, but Hell to be in!

(Signed) Andrew McKenzie Munn

6 Battalion Seaforth Highlanders

Dunkirk 1940

Transferred RAF 1941

Tail Gunner Aircrew (Lancaster's)

Killed in Action April 1943

Buried Le Mans Paris

Notes:

The Lee-Brown crew were involved in an incident during a fighter affiliation demonstration on 27 February 1943 when they were forced to bale out, the instructor, Flight Lieutenant Richard Noel Stubbs RAFVR, DFC DFM was sadly killed. At a height of 6000 ft, F/L Stubbs was demonstrating violent evasive action in Avro Lancaster W4857. During this the port fin collapsed inward and struck the port elevator which became detached. F/L Stubbs headed the aircraft back to base and ordered the crew to bale out.

Stubbs attempted to land at RAF Elsham Wolds, aborted and then climbed steeply during which the starboard fin and elevator collapsed. The aircraft dived into the ground and burst into flames killing the pilot.

The crew who parachuted from the damaged aircraft were given a Caterpillar Club pin.

F/L Stubbs was a very experienced pilot who had completed 2 tours with RAF 75 Squadron and RAF 9 Squadron. At the time of the crash, he was attached to the Air Fighting Development Unit.

Flight Sergeant James Joseph O'Brien was awarded the Distinguished Flying Medal on 25 April 1941 whilst serving with RAF 77 Squadron. He joined the RAF in 1937 at RAF Cranwell as a boy entrant.

A German night fighter flown by Lt Josef Pützkuhl (10./NJG 5) flying from Morlaix Airfield in Brittany, France claimed to have shot down a Lancaster over northern France – possibly it was a Lancaster that ditched in the English Channel.

Leslie Hore-Belisha is still widely associated in the UK with the amber "Belisha beacons" which were installed at pedestrian crossings while he was Minister for Transport.

ROYAL AIR FORCE BOMBER COMMAND, 1941-1945 (CH 9030) Avro Lancaster B Mark III, ED724 'PM-M', of No. 103 Squadron RAF pauses on the flarepath at Elsham Wolds, Lincolnshire, before taking off for a raid on Duisburg, Germany, during the Battle of the Ruhr. Three searchlights (called 'Sandra' lights), two of which are visible on the left, form a cone to indicate the height of the cloud base for the departing aircraft. Copyright: © IWM. Original Source: http://www.iwm.org.uk/collections/item/object/20521294

ROYAL AIR FORCE BOMBER COMMAND, 1942-1945. (CH 8971) The pilot of an Avro Lancaster of No. 103 Squadron RAF based at Elsham Wolds, Lincolnshire, wearing his oxygen mask while flying the aircraft at high altitude. Copyright: © IWM. Original Source: http://www.iwm.org.uk/collections/item/object/205210938

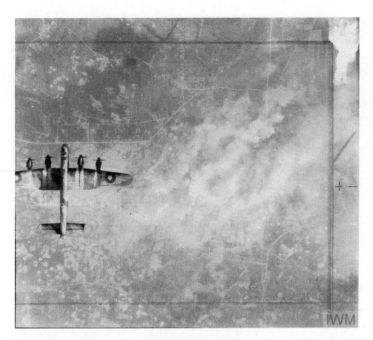

ROYAL AIR FORCE BOMBER COMMAND, 1942-1945. (C 4505) Vertical aerial photograph taken during the evening attack on the V2 assembly and launching bunker at Wizernes, France by aircraft of No. 1 Group. An Avro Lancaster of No. 103 Squadron RAF flys over the target area, which is covered by the smoke from high-explosive and incendiary bombs. Copyright: © IWM. Original Source: http://www.iwm.org.uk/collections/item/object/205023326

ROYAL AIR FORCE BOMBER COMMAND, 1942-1945. (C 3697) Annotated section of a vertical aerial photograph taken during a night raid on the docks at La Spezia, Italy. An Avro Lancaster is silhouetted over the target area as a photoflash bomb (centre right) illuminates the docks below, revealing a 'Littorio' class battleship lying in harbour ('A'). Copyright: © IWM. Original Source: http://www.iwm.org.uk/collections/item/object/205211427

ROYAL AIR FORCE BOMBER COMMAND, 1942-1945. (C 3697) Annotated section of a vertical aerial photograph taken during a night raid on the docks at La Spezia, Italy. An Avro Lancaster is silhouetted over the target area as a photoflash bomb (centre right) illuminates the docks below, revealing a 'Littorio' class battleship lying in harbour ('A'). Copyright: © IWM. Original Source: http://www.iwm.org.uk/collections/item/object/205211427

15 Flight Lieutenant Ernie 'Sherl-E' Holmes, DFC

Originally formed during the Great War, No. 35 Squadron RAF was an elite squadron within No. 8 (Pathfinder) Group RAF. Along with Nos 79, 98, 99, 234, and 264 Squadrons RAF, No. 35 Squadron RAF was known as 'Madras Presidency' as the funding for the squadrons came from the Madras Province, then an administrative subdivision of British India. Equipped with cutting-edge navigation aids and flares, the Pathfinders were charged with providing target marking ahead of (and during) bombing missions. Trained at RAF Perth in 1941, Flying Officer Ernie Holmes was a pilot with No. 35 Squadron RAF. He was shot down over Holland in May 1944.

At 10:47 hours, on Monday, 22 May 1944, Holmes's Avro Lancaster Mk III (ND762) lifted off from RAF Graveley, Cambridgeshire. It was equipped with state-of-the-art technology including Gee, Nav Aid Y (H2S – airborne ground-scanning radar system developed during the Second World War that remained in use until 1993), IFF (Identification, Friend or Foe), GPI (Ground Position Indicator), Fishpond (display unit) and Carpet, and carried 2 x LB TI (Target Indicator coloured sky marking flare) Green, 2 x TI Green, and 6 x 1,000-pound, 2 x 500 pound and 1 x 4,000-pound munitions. Its designated Pathfinder role was as a 'Visual Centrer' offering back-up targeting within the main bomber stream.

That night, 361 Lancasters and 14 Mosquitos of 1, 3, 6 and 8 Groups, were carrying out the first large raid on Dortmund (and Brunswick) for over a year and the last until after D-Day. The route was to Flamborough, 5315N 0330E, 5307N 0445E, 5212N 0715E, Target, 5110N 0734E, 5100N 0625E, 5143N 0450E, Orfordness. The raid concentrated on the south-eastern residential districts of Dortmund.

Eighteen Avro Lancasters were lost on the Dortmund raid, about 5 per cent of the total bombing force including that piloted by Holmes. On board ND762 was an 8-man crew, which had flown many missions together, always in the spirit of the squadron's motto, 'Uno Animo Agimus' ('We Act with One Accord'):

• *Ernie 'Sherl-E' Holmes (22) – pilot.*

• *John Kennedy Stewart (33) – navigator.*

• *Derrick Ernest Coleman (19) – air bomber.*

• *Frank Joseph Tudor (21) – wireless operator.*

• *Albert William Cox, age 21- air gunner.*

• *Alistair Stuart McLaren (37) – air gunner (a former Metropolitan Police officer).*

• *John Robert Cursiter (20) – flight engineer.*

The standard Avro Lancaster Mk III 7-man crew was complemented by Flying Officer Harold Thomas

Maskell (35) – reserve air bomber and wireless operator.

The Lancaster was homeward bound, flying at 16,000 feet, when it was engaged by a German night fighter. A brief attack ended at 01:29 hours when the Lancaster exploded, killing 5 of the crew members, throwing out 3 of the crew with their parachutes, all of whom reached the ground alive. The debris from the bomber fell between Middelbeers (Noord Brabant) and Vessem, 14 km west of the centre of Eindhoven in Holland killing the 5 other crew members.

Luftwaffe night fighter pilot, Oberleutnant Heinz-Wolfgang Schnaufer claimed that he shot down 4-engine ND762 3 km northwest of Eindhoven at 01:15 hours. Schnaufer, known as the 'Spook of St. Trond' after his unit's Belgian headquarters, became the most successful night fighter pilot of all time. In total, he claimed 121 shot down during the Second World War – most of his kills were RAF 4-engine bombers.

Holmes and Coleman initially evaded capture and aided by Dutch locals went underground. They were both captured in Antwerp on 17 June 1944, interrogated by the Gestapo and confined in a POW camp until the end of the war.

Warrant Officer Frank Tudor, the other survivor, collided with a tree during his descent suffering concussion and a broken leg, which necessitated urgent medical assistance. Tudor, whose DFM had been gazetted on 15 February 1944, received treatment at Oirschot. Subsequently, he surrendered to the police post in Middelbeers and thereafter was transferred (the same day) to the Feldgendarmerie (military police unit) in Eindhoven. From Eindhoven he was taken to the Luftwaffe hospital in Amsterdam where he was nursed until 31 May 1944 before being interned in a POW camp.

As the Allies and the Red Army advanced into Axis held territories, prisoners were force marched to other POW camps. In the bitter cold winter of 1944, Holmes and his fellow prisoners were made to walk hundreds of miles. In their 'Liberation Questionnaires', which were completed as part of the POW repatriation process at 106 Personnel Reception Centre (RAF Cosford) in 1945, Holmes and Coleman shared the following information:

- *E. Holmes/D. E. Colman*

- *Evaded – 22.5.1944 to 17.6.1944 – betrayed.*

- *Captured – Antwerp 17.6.1944.*

- *Imprisoned – Stalag Luft III, Sagan July 1944-January 1945.*

- *Imprisoned – Marlag und Milag Nord, Westertimke (Tarmstedt) February 1945-April 1945.*

- *Repatriated – May 1945.*

Commonwealth War Graves Commission records detail that the remains of Stewart, Maskell, Cox, McLaren, and Cursiter were concentrated (reinterred) at Eindhoven (Woensel) General Cemetery:

• *McLaren, Alistair Stuart – sergeant (1891777) – plot KK, grave 55.*

• *Cox, Albert William – flight sergeant (1314241) – plot KK, grave 56.*

• *Stewart, John Kennedy – flight lieutenant (129742) – plot KK, grave 57.*

• *Maskell, Harold Thomas – flying officer (139295)– plot KK, grave 58.*

• *Cursiter, John Robert – sergeant (1570690) plot KK, grave 70.*

During Holmes's training at RAF Perth, he met a local woman, Irene Spinks. The couple married at the West Church (today St Matthew's Church) in 1946. The early years of their married life were spent on various RAF bases. They returned to Perth in 1954 when Holmes became a flight instructor for the University of Glasgow Air Squadron, and later joined the air squadron of the University of St Andrews. Holmes left the RAF in 1962 to join Airwork Services at Scone Aerodrome as a civilian flight instructor, after which he and his wife moved to Nairobi, Kenya (and then Soroti, Uganda), where Holmes worked for East African Airways.

During this time, Holmes started having significant troubles with his vision and had to give up flying. On returning to Perth, he qualified as a social worker working, in the main, in HMP Perth. Irene became Registrar of the Aberdeen Angus Association. The platinum wedding anniversary couple moved into Kincarrathie House (residential care home), Perth, in 2016. Despite being registered as blind due to his deteriorating eyesight, a week after moving into the care home, Holmes was treated to a flight from Scone Aerodrome by Donal Foley, a former student.

Notes: Holmes's nickname, 'Sherl-E' was a Sherlock Holmes reference, a compliment to his 'pathfinding' skills. The addition of the 'E' was required to differentiate him from someone else who had the moniker 'Sherl'.

Ernie was an Avro Lancaster pilot during WW2. Not just any pilot, he was one of the best, an elite Pathfinder in RAF 35 Squadron and he is immensely proud of that accomplishment. Pathfinders located and marked the targets with flares, guiding in the main bomber force. They were also later referred to as the "master bomber".

Ernie's nickname was "Sherl-E" (Sherlock Holmes), this was given to him as a compliment to his skill in finding the target.

Ernie's DFC (= Distinguished Flying Cross) was awarded to him the day before his last bombing mission in 1944.

Ernie was awarded, Membership as a Chevalier of the Légion d'Honneur, this was given on his 99th Birthday.

Stalag Luft III where he was a POW, is the same camp that had the earlier Great and the Wooden Horse Escapes. Sandy Gunn from Auchterarder was also there, (killed by the Gestapo after the Great Escape) and Bill Reid VC from Crieff was imprisoned there as well.

Sergeant Alistair Stuart McLaren, who was Ernie's Air Gunner on Avro Lancaster ND762 and killed that day in 1944, was born at 14 Robertson's Buildings, Perth (opposite the Police Station). Ernie visited the family I believe after the war.

After the war, Ernie became a flying instructor and miraculously survived two further aircraft crashes. (Ernie survived aircraft crashes every 10 years, in 1944, 1954 and 1964)

Ernie and his pupil Cadet Pilot J. Mustarde from Campbelltown "bailed out" by parachute of a Chipmunk aircraft on 23 September 1954. The aircraft crashed in a field near Errol. It came down with such force much of it was buried. An eyewitness and first on the scene, was a 29-year-old German dairyman, Wolfgang Kosanetzki, oddly, he was a former Luftwaffe pilot during WW2.

Ernie was the instructor on 24 June 1964 in a twin-engine Cessna 310, which crashed shortly after take-off from Scone. Two trainee Iraq pupils were on-board – Kamil Aljarrah and Rayadh al-Freeig. The aircraft skimmed over the airfield boundary fence and ploughed into a field containing prize bulls. Ernie was admitted to Bridge of Earn Hospital with severe burns to face and hand. His condition was said to be "only fair". The others "fairly comfortable".

Memorial for the crashed Lancaster ND762

FIFTH

MELROSO
REFRESHING FROM PURE GRAPE JUICE

| HIGH STRENGTH WINE | HIGH IN VITAMINS WINE |
| Fortified with spirit. PER BOTT. 9/6 | PER BOTT. 6/- |

ng Telegraph and Post.

...up, 9.12 p.m.; Moon, 2.42 a.m.-5.42 p.m.

EE, THURSDAY, SEPTEMBER 23, 1954.   1½d

The two fliers are seen on the right, with the man in white overalls.

Two Bale Out Of Crashing Plane

Instructor and pupil baled out when their R.A.F. Chipmunk trainer nose-dived out of control into a field on the south side of the Dundee-Perth road today. The crash occurred opposite Melville's Garage, Half-Way House.

The fliers were Flight Lieutenant Ernest Holmes Oakley, 42 Jeanfield Road, Perth, and Cadet-Pilot James Mustard (18), 107 Ralston Road, Campbeltown, Argyll. Flight Lieutenant Holmes escaped with a knee injury, while his pupil was uninjured. This was Mustard's first jump.

The plane was from Glasgow University Air Squadron flying from Scone.

The occupants drifted down about 50 yards from their wrecked plane and were able to walk unassisted from the field. They were given a cup of tea in the house of Mr Kenneth Melville, garage proprietor, while word of the accident was sent to Scone.

Mr Melville was in his office when he heard a bang, looked out and saw the wreckage. "It kind had a bird," said Mr Melville, "but just after that I saw the two parachutes coming down."

Today's accident happened about a quarter of a mile distant from the scene of a fatal jet fighter crash in March.

An eye-witness was 29-year-old German dairyman, Wolfgang ...., employed at Balgillom Dairy, ... Road. He was first on the scene at the March mishap.

Wolfgang, an enthusiastic pilot, said he had been watching the plane doing aerobatics. "Could you do that?" asked his young cadet son as the plane dived, tipped around, and then shot up again.

So, replied Wolfgang, who admitted he had always been quite happy to stay on even keel. His particular branch of flying was artillery spotting in a Focke-Wulf on the Italian front.

As they continued to watch, the Chipmunk went into another dive, but this time continued to spin down to earth. His impression was that the crew had held on until the last moment in an effort to right it before jumping.

Cattle grazing in the field escaped injury.

16 Murie Cemetery, Fairey Swordfish, and the River Tay

The RAF opened an airfield by the village of Errol, within the Carse of Gowrie, midway between Dundee and Perth, on 1 August 1942. Operations at RAF Errol commenced with the transfer of No. 9 (P)AFU from RAF Hullavington in Wiltshire and No. 21 AFU, which was posted there on 9 August 1942.

The station's RAF complement included 67 officers, 116 SNCOs, 1682 ORs – its WAAF complement included 10 officers, 15 SNCOs and 405 ORs. There were 6 Type 1 hangars and 13 blister hangars, 17 concrete hard standings (circular), 3 runways arranged in an 'A' orientation of lengths 1,600 yards, 1,180 yards, and 1,170 yards. No. 21 AFU maintained a complement of 37 pilots, 9 of whom were from New Zealand.

Units using RAF Errol during the Second World War include:

No. 9 EGS (Elementary Gliding School).

No. 9 (P)AFU (Navy pilot training unit relocated from

RAF Hullavington, Wiltshire).

No. 260 MU, No. 271 Squadron RAF.

No. 810 Squadron RNFAA.

No. 1544 BAT Flight (Blind (later Beam) Approach Training Flight).

No. 1680 (Transport) Flight RAF

Arthur A. J. Roberton was born on 12.03.14, in Westmount, Quebec, Canada to Lewis Alexander Roberton (of Govan, near Glasgow) and Mary (nee Pearson), also born in Scotland. Arthur's parents were married in Montreal on 17.05.06 and Arthur was the third child (and second son), all of whom were born in Canada.

Arthur was baptised (as a Presbyterian) in Montreal on 19.03.14. His father, Lewis Snr, was a chartered accountant, who died on 30.03.16 aged 49 years, shortly after Arthur's second birthday. Mary and her three children arrived back in Glasgow, on board the Athenia, on 29.10.16.

Arthur's mother remarried in 1933, when Arthur was 19, to Douglas Graham in Hillhead, Glasgow.

Arthur spent much of his schooldays at Hillhead High School except for a short period at Liverpool Collegiate. He attended the Universities of both Edinburgh and Glasgow, studying the Arts at Glasgow from 1931 – 34 and 1937 – 39, then decided – according to the honour roll of Glasgow University – to enter the Church, though there was no further evidence to substantiate this. Towards the end of 1941, Arthur joined the Fleet Air Arm and was trained at Kingston, Ontario, Canada, where he won his "wings" and was commissioned. He became a temporary acting Sub-Lieutenant on 30.12.42. Also in 1942, in

Hillhead, Glasgow, Arthur married Sarah Beattie McNaughton Tait, from Kirkintilloch, who was aged 19 at the time of their wedding (Arthur was 28).

After training, Arthur was posted on 22.02.43, for further instruction and flying duties to Errol in Scotland; to Crail Aerodrome, also known as HMS Jackdaw. Royal Naval Air Station Crail or RNAS Crail (HMS Jackdaw) was located 4.9 miles (7.9 km) of Anstruther, Fife and 8.8 miles (14.2 km) of St Andrews. The Royal Navy had commissioned the Errol airfield on 1 October 1940 as HMS Jackdaw for use as a TBR (Torpedo Bomber Reconnaissance) base. Many units visited Crail for varying lengths of time including brief stays from aircraft carriers and longer durations for training. Crail's location gave quick accessibility to the sea ranges in the Firth of Forth and Navy ships with which to train, making the airfield ideal as a base for torpedo training especially.

Arthur is listed as being part of 9 (Pilots) Advanced Flying Unit and, at this stage of WW2, his training (after having received his wings) could have been expected to last 4 – 6 weeks. Tragically, he would appear to have been only about 4 weeks into this advanced training, whilst on an exercise from HMS Jackdaw that he met his death. The University of Glasgow memorial site records that he was flying in close formation over the Firth of Tay when his aircraft came into contact with another and both crashed, with fatal results to the occupants. The aeroplane Arthur was reported at the time as flying in was a Miles Master two-seater training aircraft.

Royal Navy Reserve Sub-Lieutenant **Arthur Allan Jackson Roberton** is in fact cited in conjunction with Royal Navy Volunteer Reserve Sub-Lt **Bertram Henry Prance** on several reports, as both having died on the same day. Sub-Lt Roberton and Sub-Lt Prance were in fact the pilots of two Fairey Swordfish biplane torpedo bombers on 19 March 1943 which collided and interlocked above the River Tay near Longforgan. No other individuals were listed as having died on that date on the graves' registration record. Sub-Lieutenant Arthur A.J. Roberton was flying Fairey Swordfish I V4380, Sub Lieutenant Bertram H. Prance was flying Fairey Swordfish II DK781.

It should be noted that whilst Arthur was listed as having been serving with the RAF, in 9th Pilot Advanced Flying Unit, Sub-Lt Prance was reported as having been serving with the Fleet Air Arm, in 834 Sqn. Both were still officially listed at the time of their death as assigned to HMS Jackdaw. Whilst Arthur was listed on the Royal Navy casualty lists – Sub-Lt Prance was not.

Arthur was survived by both his siblings, despite his brother – a lieutenant in the Royal Artillery – having had to survive the rigors of a Japanese P.O.W. camp. Brother Lewis died in Montreal in 1994 and sister Mary in Glasgow in 1990. No reliable evidence of a date of death for Arthur's mother could be located. Arthur's wife Sarah died in Kelvin on 23.08.61 and no evidence of her re-marrying or of any children could be located at this time.

Betram age 24, was the son of Henry Aylett Prance and Cissie Elizabeth Prance and the husband of Maude Evelyn Prance of Colney Hatch, Middlesex, England

Bertram Henry Prance was born on 31st March 1918, the first (and only) son of Harry Aylett Prance and his wife, Cissie Elizabeth (nee Elsdon). Bertram was the youngest of four children. Bertram was five years old when his father died in 1923, at aged 40. His mother remarried (to Henry Snell) in 1928, when Bertram was around ten years old, and Henry was fifty-three.

On 28th October 1935, Bertram joined the police force, aged 17 years (though one site lists him as having joined on 7th February 1938). His warrant number was 126666 and he appears to have served in both G and Y Divisions, which accounts for the anomaly in dating, if 1938 was the time at which he transferred divisions. One set of police records identifies him as having left on 19th March 1943 (his passing), so it is feasible that he remained "on the books" of the police force until that time (see below).

In 1939, Bertram was recorded as living at 40 Beak Street, London W1. His occupation was given as 'police constable'. On the same register, two of his three sisters (Katie and Marjorie) were listed as living in Orchard Cottages, Richmond in the North Riding of Yorkshire. Both Katie and Marjorie were married at this time; Katie's husband was a 'farm pig man' and Marjorie was recorded as living with them.

On the eve of the war there were some 60,000 police officers in England and Wales divided between 182 separate police forces. The largest force was the Metropolitan Police in London with just under 20,000 men; there was a separate force for the City of London (1,100 men). There were fifty-eight county forces and 122 forces patrolling cities and boroughs. (There were fewer than three hundred women in the total of 60,000. Policing was seen as a man's job. Women police officers were largely confined to dealing with family problems and particularly with women and children.)

The advent of war meant that young men were required to fight in the conflict, but the situation also required reservists – men who had recently been soldiers – to return to the army or navy since trained men were essential. Many police officers were reservists, and many more were young enough to serve in the armed forces. This meant that, at the outset of the war, police numbers were reduced as reservists returned to their units and as young police officers volunteered for military service. The government and the police authorities sought to limit the reduction in police officers by restricting the numbers who might volunteer. Police ranks were made up by recruiting reserve policemen, special constables, and more women officers. In the closing months of 1939, 3,000 reservists left the police forces to serve in their former military units. Over the course of the war another 16,500 policemen volunteered for the army, navy, or air force; of these 1,275 were killed or died while on active service.

Policemen who were military reservists had been called up at the start of the war. The more formal use of 'reserved occupations' in the Second World War did include policemen. However, manpower shortages by 1942 meant policemen under twenty-five were conscripted. As Bertram did not leave the police force (to enlist) till 10th July 1942, aged 24 years. It is therefore possible that he had been conscripted.

Bertram married Maude (elsewhere spelt 'Maud') Evelyn Elizabeth Stonehouse (also incorrectly cited as 'Storehouse' on one occasion) in 1940. Maude had been born in Edmonton, Middlesex on 29th October 1915. The couple were married in the same locale. There is no evidence of children from this marriage.

All three of Bertram's sisters outlived him, dying in the 21st century. His mother Cissie also outlived him, dying in 1974 in Brixworth, Northamptonshire; her second husband having passed away in 1948 also in Brixworth. This would appear to suggest that at least most of the family had moved to the north of England at some stage. (His sister Ivy died in Enfield, Middlesex.)

Bertram's probate record, registered on 6th September 1943 in Llandudno, leaves a total of £832.11.2d to his widow, Maude Prance. At the time of that deposition, his address was cited as 39 St Ivian Court, Muswell Hill, Middlesex. Maud remarried, to Geoffrey D. Kay, in 1945.

Bertram was reported as having been serving with the Fleet Air Arm, in 834 Sqn at the time of the incident in which he lost his life, having been seconded to No.9 (Pilots) A.F.U. Course RAF Errol for further training. No further details of his service since the time of his enlistment have been unearthed at this time.

Bertram is interred in Murie cemetery, beside his comrade (Sub-Lt Roberton), in a section designated for those who served with HMS Jackdaw.

Two days before Arthur and Bertram's mid-air collision, a Miles Master T8768 belly-landed at Errol.

Temporary Acting Sub-Lieutenant **John Roland Hobday**, Royal Navy Volunteer Reserve, HMS Macaw, age 19, was killed on 30 March 1944. Sub-Lieutenant Hobday died as the result of an air crash whilst flying with RAF 9(P)AFU Errol.

John Roland Hobday was born on 12.07.24, in Walsall, Staffordshire, England to Harold and Sarah (nee Wootton). John's mother died in April 1936, a few months before John's 12th birthday. John's father appears to have remarried within three months of his mother's passing, to Joan (nee Cullerne) and it is Joan who is memorialised on his gravestone. John's half-brother, Peter, was born in 1940.

John attended Moseley Grammar School, near Birmingham from 1935 till 1940. No information could be found about his life from then until 12.01.44, when John – as a member of the Royal Naval Voluntary Reserve – became a Temporary Acting Sub-Lieutenant, at which time he was noted as serving with H.M.S. Macaw, as part of the Fleet Air Arm. However, as he has been noted to have spent time at Wellbank in Cumberland before his promotion to Sub-Lieutenant, it is considered likely that he would have – prior to this – undergone pilot training in Canada.

The Wellbank Hostel, as it was known, had been built in 1941-42 on land requisitioned by the Ministry of Supply near Bootle Station, to house five hundred workers engaged in the construction of the Royal Ordnance Factory at Hycemoor. It was transferred to the Admiralty in November 1943 and work began to adapt the site as a transit camp where new Fleet Air Arm Pilots were to assemble on their return to the UK after completing their preliminary flying training in the Service Flying Training Schools in Canada. The hostel was commissioned on November 17th, 1943, as H.M.S. Macaw and, initially, the ship's accounts were carried by the Naval Air Station at Inskip, H.M.S. Nightjar, before becoming an independent command on New Year's Day 1944, less than a fortnight before John was commissioned.

Although no records were discovered of John's service prior to him joining H.M.S. Macaw, it would not seem unreasonable to assume that his career path followed the "standard route". Trainee pilots left the UK for Canada as Leading Naval Airmen, having completed their preliminary, non-flying training at HMS St Vincent in Gosport. On arrival back in the UK, those qualified as pilots reported to HMS Macaw where they attended the Admiralty Interview Board, which comprised a panel of senior naval officers, to decide their suitability to become an officer in Royal Navy Volunteer Reserve (Air Branch). Those under 19½ would become a Temporary Acting Midshipman RNVR, whilst those over 19½ – like John – would become a Temporary Acting Sub Lieutenant RNVR. The newly commissioned officers were then sent on two weeks leave, during which time they would attend a Naval Tailors and be fitted for uniforms. On return to HMS MACAW any deficiencies in their flying equipment and other kit would be rectified from stores held on site in preparation for appointment to their next stage of flying training in the UK.

In John's case, he began his documented service with HMS Macaw on 07.02.44 and was sent to 9 (Pilot) Advanced Flying Unit based at Errol, Perth, where he was killed just over a month later.

John died on 30.03.44, at the age of nineteen. Various sources report that he was flying a Miles Magister T8559 from RAF Errol when the aircraft became "iced up" during a night flight exercise and had to be abandoned, subsequently crashing into the river Tay near Newburgh in Fife. John bailed out before the crash but did not survive. His body was recovered from the river on 11th May, 42 days after the crash.

John is interred in Murie Cemetery, where his headstone states he is "remembered with honour". (On this stone, as previously mentioned, Joan is recorded as his mother, though her name is recorded as 'Joan Pease Hobday', whilst her middle name is Pearl).

John was survived by his father, stepmother, and brother.

RAF Sergeant Pilot (Instructor) 1345409 Charles Muirhead, 9 (P)AFU RAF Errol, was reported as killed on active service on 25 January 1943. Age 21 he was the only son of Mr and Mrs Douglas Muirhead, Palacehill, near the village of Ancrum in the Borders. It is not confirmed but is suggested that he was the pilot of Miles Master Mk.I T8398 which flew into high ground at Balluderon Hill near Auchterhouse, north of Dundee. Balluderon Hill is beside the popular Balkello Community Woodland Park managed by the Forestry Commission. Sergeant Muirhead is buried in Murie Cemetery, Errol.

Sub-Lieutenant Winston Veron Stark, Royal New Zealand Reserve, HMS Macaw, age 20, died on 7 March 1943. He was the son of George Harry and Eliza Stark of Havelock North, Hawke's Bay, New Zealand, formerly of Leicestershire, England. After training at HMNZS Philomel, Devonport Dockyard, Auckland, New Zealand, Winston left New Zealand in October 1941 to join the Fleet Air Arm. On arrival in the UK, he transferred to HMS St. Vincent, shore establishment in Gosport and was sent on to 9(P)AFU at Errol. After advance flight training, he was posted to HMS Jackdaw at Crail. Winston was flying Hawker Hurricane V6786 when on 7 March 1943 it crashed into Loch Leven near Kinross. The crash was recorded as 'unauthorised low flying'. Sub-Lieutenant Stark is buried in Murie Cemetery, Errol. Winston's parents George and Eliza Stark did later visit his grave and Loch Leven.

Sergeant Pilot William (Billy) Edmonstone Woodington, R/112242, Royal Canadian Air Force, age 19, was killed on 29 December 1942. He was the son of Leslie and Jean Woodington of Kensington, Prince Edward Island, Canada. Sergeant Woodington was born in Scotland; they went to Canada in October 1942 where he was a student. Billy Woodington was killed when his a Miles Master monoplane advanced trainer aircraft from 9 (P)AFU at RAF Errol crashed near Rossie Priory, Inchture. He is buried in Murie Cemetery, Errol.

A Soviet Armstrong Whitworth Albemarle ST1 P1503 on a training flight from Errol, crashed near to Fearnan, Loch Tay on 29 May 1943 killing the crew of three. Also onboard was Staff Sergeant Frantisek Drahovazal a 34-year-old cook in the Czechoslovakian Army from Trutnov (Czeck Republic) who wished to take an aerial excursion before the end of his tour in Scotland. He lies in Murie Cemetery, Errol.

Notes:

Although they may not have seen active service per se, Arthur, John and Bertram's volunteering spirit is deserving of honour and respect. These two brave men, both of whom had lost their fathers at an early age, may have been buried at a distance from their homes and loved ones but they are not forgotten. Lest we forget.

Fairey Swordfish K8407 collided with a Tiger Moth BB685 on 23 December 1942 at Balhepburn Farm, near Elcho Castle, Rhynd (Where Sky and Summit Meet (2019), Ken Bruce). Swordfish K8407 was delivered to the packing depot at RAF Sealand, south of Liverpool on 29 December 1936. This was where aircraft were crated before (usually) being sent overseas. It was then assigned to 824 Squadron in April 1937 until October 1941. It spent some time at RAF White Waltham and RNAS Lee (on Solent) until was transferred to 9 (P)AFU at Errol in April 1942. Swordfish K8407 is not listed as being lost due to the accident, one report suggested the pilot was killed, this is unconfirmed. The assumption must be that this aircraft survived the crash and returned to its base, probably RAF Errol.

RNAS 824 Squadron took part in Operation Judgement, the Battle of Taranto on 11 November 1940, 5 aircraft being transferred to new HMS Illustrious from the elderly HMS Eagle (launched 1918) which was having its leaking aviation fuel system repaired. 824 along with 813, 815, and 819 squadrons were involved in the battle.

Fairey Swordfish P4267 from 9 (P)AFU at Errol on 14 November 1942 had an engine failure and force landed at Balhelvie Farm just east of Newburgh. The aircraft nosed over at speed; Sub-Lieutenant P. T. Gifford was unhurt. William Wallace fought a skirmish with the English, Earl of Pembroke in 1298 near here, at the battle of Black Earnside.

Fairey Swordfish Mk. I, W5856 which was at RAF Errol in 1943 and 1944 was restored to fly again from a badly corroded condition at Sir William Roberts Strathallan Aircraft Museum near Auchterarder. Swordfish W5856 is the oldest surviving in the world. She first flew on 21 October 1941 and was delivered to 82 MU (Maintenance Unit) at RAF Lichfield for overseas transport to Gibraltar on board the SS Empire Morn. After a year she returned to Fairey's Stockport factory for refurbishment in the winter of 1942/43. On 14 April 1943, W5856 was assigned to 9 (P)AFU at RAF Errol. After a temporary short loan in February 1944 to RAF Manston for tactical trials, she returned to join C Flight at 9 (P)AFU and suffered an engine failure on take-off from RAF Errol on Sunday 5 March 1944. W8586 crashed through the road on the north side of the aerodrome. The pilot was Sub-Lieutenant S. T. Brand who was unhurt. It was repaired at 76 MU RAF Wroughton on 11 July 1944, and it was known to be in transit between Hamble and Eastleigh on 18 July 1944. On 15 October 1944 it went to 1 Naval Air Gunners School at RCAF Yarmouth on the Isle of Wight. It was taken on strength by Canada on 15 December 1944. She was sent to storage in April 1945 at RCAF Mount Hope (Hamilton Ontario), where she was again used in the training role. Struck off charge on 21 August 1946, W8586 was sold as war assets. It was bought by an Ontario man and stored on a farm until it was re-sold to a J. F. Carter from Monroeville, Alabama, USA, for use as a crop duster. It was next bought by the Strathallan collection and arrived there in crates on 7 August 1977.

British Aerospace at Brough acquired W8586 for reconstruction in 1991 and following a successful test flight in 1993 she was gifted to the Royal Navy Historic Flight. Three years later was adopted by the City of Leeds, in tribute to the local companies that built Swordfish components during WWII. She now wears the City's coat of arms and name on her port side just forward of the pilot's cockpit. Grounded with corrosion in her wing spars in 2003, a new set of wings were delivered in 2012 and W8586 re-joined the display circuit in 2015. It now carries a new paint scheme depicting a Swordfish of 820 Naval Air Squadron during the attack on the Bismarck in 1941.

Royal Navy 820 Naval Air Squadron's Lieutenant Commander John William Charlton Moffat, piloting a Fairey Swordfish on 26 May 1941, is recognised as being responsible for crippling the Kreigsmarine (Nazi Germany's navy) battleship Bismarck by hitting the ship in the rudder-steering area. John Moffat resided in Dunkeld for several years and passed away at Viewlands House care home in Perth on 11 December 2016 (Where Sky and Summit Meet (2019), Ken Bruce & I Sank the Bismarck (2010) John Moffat). A later Mk.III Fairey Swordfish NF389 was one of two used during the filming of the 1960 movie, Sink the Bismarck staring Kenneth More.

Sub-Lieutenant John Weatherhead from Pitlochry flew Swordfish K8586 at RAF Errol in 1943. On the first occasion on 24 June 1943, he flew K8586 for one hour and 10 minutes, on the second occasion two days later for 35 minutes when he brought it back from RNAS Crail (Jackdaw). After completing basic flying training, he was sent to 9 (P)AFU at RAF Errol to convert to the Fairey Swordfish. He moved on to RNAS Crail for weapons training, followed by a spell at East Haven (HMS Peewit, between Carnoustie and Arbroath) for carrier deck landing. HMS Peewit was commissioned on 1 May 1943 and closed in July 1946. During WW2, John Weatherhead flew 375 hours in Fairey Swordfish, 108 of those on anti-submarine hours with Fleet Air Arm 836 Squadron. He notched up sixty-seven deck landings (four at night) flying from Merchant aircraft carrier (MAC) ships. These were converted grain or tanker ships with a makeshift flight deck installed. They could carry up to four Swordfish aircraft or six Hawker Hurricane fighters whilst still maintaining its cargo-carrying capacity. John Weatherhead when he retired stayed in Bonnethill Road, Pitlochry.

Upon the closure of the Strathallan collection, one of its display aircraft, a de Havilland Vampire found its way to a collector who stored it at Errol Airfield.

Seven paratroopers drowned on 13 June 1943 at Wormit Bay during a training exercise. Two Armstrong Whitely bombers approached from the south at about 4.00pm. Winds were gusting up to 30 mph and 18 fully laden paratroopers of the 8th Battalion (Midland Counties) The Parachute Regiment landed in the river. RAF air sea rescue launches, and the Broughty Ferry RNLI lifeboat took part in the rescue. One of the two planes contained Polish troops who landed in shallow water and survived.

These two aircraft were part of a ten Armstrong Whitley parachute drop exercise, carrying in total 130 troops were about 10 miles west of their intended drop zone at Tentsmuir, near Leuchars. One paratrooper at Wormit Bay refused to jump and was later court-martialled. At Tentsmuir, a paratrooper was struck during the jump by an ammunition box and killed.

In the River Tay Estuary opposite Dundee between Woodhaven, Newport and Tayport on 6 October 1938, the Short Brothers-Mayo (Maia & Mercury) composite flying boat/seaplane aircraft (piggy-backed aircraft) set off to establish a record seaplane flight to South Africa. The two aircraft comprised the Short S.21 Maia (G-ADHK) and the Short S.20 Mercury (G-ADHJ). They separated over the Dundee Law and Captain Donald C.T. Bennett (later to be founder of the Pathfinder bomber force) and his co-pilot Ian Harvey, proceeded to fly 6,045 miles in Mercury in 42 hours 26 minutes to the estuary of the Orange River, just short of their destination at Cape Town.

Sunderland Flying Boats of 210 Squadron arrived at Tayport around the same time being transferred as a precaution during the Munich Crisis. They did not stay long and transferred on to Wales on 8 October 1938.

In February 1942, No. 333 (Norwegian) Squadron RAF, a detachment of No. 1477 (Norwegian) Flight arrived at Woodhaven equipped with Consolidated PBY-1b (Catalina) seaplanes. This was a mixed squadron; in May 1943, a full squadron was formed from this flight, equipped with de Havilland Mosquito's Mk. II and Mk. V, based at RAF Leuchars and later RAF Banff. The Catalinas carried out anti-submarine patrols and search and rescue. They also operated in the 'Special Duties' role assisting the Norwegian Resistance. They landed agents, transmitters and even are said to have dropped Christmas presents to the Norwegian population. The squadron is still operational today and is currently based at Andøya Air Station in Nordland, Norway

During 1943 there were a series of three deception operations designed to deceive the Germans that an invasion might occur in areas such as Brest and Boulogne in France or at Stavanger in Norway. The second of three-deception operations of the plan, Operation Cockade was Operation Tindall in which RAF Errol played a part. It was conceived to suggest that the goal of the allies was a sea and air landing at Stavanger, Norway in mid-September 1943. The Germans kept back twelve army divisions in Norway to counter the potential threat. This weaking their defences in Sicily which the allies invaded 9 July 1943 – 17 August 1943 and the forces available for the German Operation Citadel, the encircling attack at the Battle of Kursk, July 1943 which was repulsed by the Soviet Red Army. Adolf Hitler eventually cancelled further attempts to break through the Soviet defences during this offensive, in part due to the news of the Allied invasion of Sicily. The soviets suffered 800,000 casualties at Kursk.

Two Armstrong Whitley A.W38 twin-engine bombers, each towing a glider landed at RAF Errol on 6 August 1943. RAF Errol at the time was a base for packing and air-dropping supplies to advancing troops using six Douglas C-47 Skytrain transport aircraft, (aka Dakotas) of RAF 271 Squadron. A pair of Airspeed As.51 Horsa I troop-carrying gliders were listed on the manifest of RAF Errol in 1943. It is conceivable that the goings on at Errol worried the Germans, a Luftwaffe reconnaissance aircraft of Luftwaffen-Führungsstab Ic (Command Staff) was detailed to photograph the Flugplatz (airfield) in April 1943.

Arthur Roberton's Fairey Swordfish V4380 was delivered from Fairey's Blackburn factory on 26 April 1941 to 812 Naval Air Squadron, one of a batch of three hundred made. It took part in Operation EF, the Raid on Kirkness and Petsamo, on 30 July 1941. During the German Operation Barbarossa, Fleet Air Arm aircraft from the aircraft carriers HMS Victorius and HMS Furious attacked merchant vessels in the northern Norwegian port of Kirkness and the north Finnish port of Liinakhamari in Petsamo. Swordfish V4380 was one of nine Swordfish along with nine Fairey Albacores that attacked Petsamo. V4380 was transferred to 779 Squadron Fleet Requirements Unit at Gibraltar which was form on 1 October 1941. In February 1942 it was back with 812 Squadron and on 8 September 1942 a tail wheel was broken on landing at RAF Docking (Norfolk). An engine failure occurred on 13 October 1942 on take-off from RAF Coltishall (Norfolk) and it appears it was then transferred up to 9 (P)AFU – (Pilots) Advanced Flying Unit) at Errol. Marked as written off following the crash at Longforgan on 19 March 1943. A notable Coltishall fighter pilot was Douglas Bader, appointed as leader of No. 242 Squadron, a mostly Canadian pilot Hurricane squadron.

Liinakhamari, Petsamo was in part of the Finnish territory that was ceded to the Soviet Union in 1944 at the conclusion of their Continuation War. Following their armistice and with pressure put on the Finns by the Soviets to actively remove the occupying German forces in Lapland, the retreating Germans adopted a scorched earth policy and laid waste to the entire Northern half of the country. 100,000 people lost their homes. The main strategic interest to the Germans was the nickel mines in the Petsamo region.

Bertram Pance's, Fairey Swordfish DK781 was delivered from Fairey's Blackburn factory on 25 April 1942, one of a batch of four hundred made. It was assigned to 834 Squadron from July 1942 to September 1942 when it was transferred 9 (P)AFU at Errol. 834 Squadron was formed at Palisades, Jamica in December 1941 as a torpedo bomber reconnaissance Swordfish squadron. They embarked on the Long Island Class escort carrier, HMS Archer which was commissioned into the Royal Navy on 6 May 1942 at Brooklyn, New York. After sailing to South Africa, HMS Archer was detailed to convoy duties to the USA and Gibraltar. DK781 was also marked as written off following the crash on 19 March 1943. Ten numbers after DK781 were designated, DK791 is now on display at the Museum of Transport and Technology in Auckland, New Zealand.

Early in 1943, three Supermarine Walrus single-engine, amphibious biplane reconnaissance aircraft were lent to RAF Errol. Despite remonstration that at least one Walrus should be retained for rescuing downed pilots in the River Tay, they were assigned elsewhere in April 1944.

RAF Errol went into maintenance mode on 26 June 1945 when 800 RAF and WAAF personnel left for Shropshire. One hundred men entrained at 2.00pm at Inchcoonans and about five hundred personnel left by train at 6.00pm from Errol Station. Perth Black Watch Pipe Band piped them on the 2½ miles from the aerodrome. The remainder flew directly to Shropshire. The daily transport service plane to RNAS Hatston (HMS Sparrowhawk) in Orkney was maintained until the RAF left the aerodrome.

Malcolm (Callum) Mitchell a resident of Kinnoull, Perth was born in 1923 and joined the Fleet Air Arm at the age of seventeen. He was commissioned as a Sub-Lieutenant a year later. In 1943 he spent five months at RAF Errol, RNAS Crail and RNAS Arbroath (HMS Condor) learning to fly the Swordfish, torpedo, and land on aircraft carrier decks. In 1944 he sank a U-boat during Russian convoys operations. He left the navy with the rank of Lieutenant Commander in 1946.

The surname Roberton was first found recorded in Lanarkshire. The village of Roberton is in South Lanarkshire, where it was the seat of the Roberton's until their dispossession by Robert the Bruce in 1296 for Stephen de Roberton's signing of the Ragman Roll (their allegiance to the English King Edward I).

Research by Ken Bruce and Sue Gibson.

Royal Navy Reserve Sub-Lieutenant Arthur Allan Jackson Roberton

Fairey Swordfish Mk. I on a training flight from Crail 1940

Billy Woodington

17 Warrant Officer William Alexander Watson DFM

Flight Engineer William Alexander Watson (567222) joined the RAF straight from school in 1934 as an apprentice at RAF Halton, near Wendover in Buckinghamshire. Watson preferred to be known as Sandy. He trained as a fitter and by 1935 he was awarded the coveted Barrington-Kennett medal for his sporting achievements.

By 1938, Watson had been promoted to Aircraftman First Class. By 1941, he had been trained in air gunnery and he was posted to RAF 15 Squadron in June 1941 (RAF 15 Squadron is also known as RAF XV Squadron). On 10 August 1941, he was promoted to sergeant on his return to the squadron following flight engineering training at Short Brothers.

Watson commenced operational flying on 7 September 1941. During take-off on a mission to bomb Berlin, one wheel of the undercarriage of his Short Stirling heavy bomber would not retract. The pilot jettisoned the bomb load at a safe location and on the final attempt, the faulty undercarriage operated correctly. The aircraft and crew landed safely.

Up until that time, Watson was a spare crew member. Flying Officer Peter Boggis, the pilot, was impressed by Watson's ability and secured him as his regular flight engineer. He was now destined to fly in the most prestigious and historically important Short Stirling bomber.

Lady Rachel Workman MacRobert of Douneside in the County of Aberdeen in memory of her three sons killed in RAF service, donated £25,000 to buy a Short Stirling bomber. It was given the serial number N6086 and had the MacRobert coat of arms painted on the nose. It was named, 'Reply' and presented to her crew at RAF Wyton on 10 October 1941. It was assigned to RAF 15 Squadron and given the code 'LS-F'.

The first operation flown by N6086 was on 12 October 1941, to bomb Nuremberg, Germany. On 28 October 1941, the 'MacRobert's Reply' sustained its first damage from anti-aircraft fire over Nieuport (Nieuwpoort), Belgium. On 18 December 1941, they took part in the attack on the German Pocket Battleship Scharnhost and Heavy Cruiser Gneisenau in the French harbour of Brest. This was their second visit, in four days, this time they hit with their bombs the dry dock where the Gneisenau was berthed and saw black smoke rising from the warship. They were attacked by Luftwaffe fighters and managed to damage one of them with their guns.

The 'MacRoberts Reply', captained by Flying Officer Peter Boggis flew on 12 operations from October 1941 to January 1942. On 7 February 1942, the aircraft veered during take-off at RAF Peterhead and collided with a damaged Supermarine Spitfire (Watson was not on board). It was repaired and flew again with conversion units before being written off in 1943.

On 26 January 1942, Watson had by now completed two tours of operations and was posted to RAF 15 Squadron Conversion Flight as an instructor. In August 1942, he was now an acting flight sergeant and returned to RAF 15 Squadron where he took part in another eleven operations. He was then posted to RAF 90 Squadron where he took part in a further fourteen operations.

Watson teamed up with another former RAF 15 Squadron pilot, Hugh 'Wendle' Wilkie from New Zealand. On 11 June 1943, they lost a propeller due to friendly fire from another Short Stirling whilst over the target area – nonetheless, they returned safely.

On the night of 18 April 1944, Short Stirling EJ108 with Watson and Wilkie took off at 22.35 hours from RAF Grafton Underwood, east of Kettering, Northamptonshire, with a crew of nine onboard, most of whom were undergoing training. Watson was now a warrant officer and were now part of RAF 1657 HCU (Heavy Conversion Unit) which was based at RAF Stradishall, between Cambridge and Bury St Edmonds. They were on a training exercise, practising night take-offs and landings (circuits and bumps). RAF Polebrook which was being used by the USAAC (United States Army Air Corp) was clear that day of any operational flying.

During a practice landing and take-off at RAF Polebrook, they hit and killed three USAAC personnel who were cycling on a runway. With damage to an engine and the possibility of damage to the undercarriage of the aircraft, they were committed to continue the take-off. As they became airborne, they were advised to land at the emergency landing strip at RAF Woodbridge, Suffolk.

Shortly before reaching RAF Woodbridge, there was an internal explosion and control of the aircraft was lost, the aircraft went into a steep nose up attitude. Six of the crew bailed out successfully, the two others were killed at 22.30pm in the crash at Moat Farm near Little Glemham 7 miles NE of Woodbrige. Sergeant Atkins died as he had failed to attach his parachute harness correctly and slipped through the webbing, subsequently plunging to his death. Two civilians, a brother and sister, Mr. W Carter and Miss Carter, whose thatched cottage was hit by part of the aircraft emerged unscathed.

Crash Location: Little Glemham, Suffolk. The crew onboard EJ108:

Flight Lieutenant Hugh Charles Wilkie RNZAF (415397) DFC, pilot, age 21

Flight Sergeant Colin George Nairne RNZAF (42117) 2nd pilot, age 22, Survived

Warrant Officer William (Sandy) Alexander Watson RAF (567222) DFM, fight engineer, age 25

Sergeant Frederick Thomas George Atkins RAFVR (1603538) flight engineer, age 20

Pilot Officer Lyndon Clifford Perry RNZAF (428925) air bomber, age 21, Survived

Pilot Officer Frederick Gerald Rickard (429366) RNZAF wireless operator/air gunner, age 22, Survived

Sergeant Alfred Richard Stannard RAFVR (1338510) wireless operator/air gunner, age 22. Survived

Sergeant Stanley Alfred George Woodford RAFVR (922095) air gunner, age 29, Survived

Flight Sergeant Philip Falkiner RNZAF (425140) air gunner, age 21, Survived

On the ground, the personnel from 545 Bomber Squadron, 384th Bomber Group, 8th Air Force. USAAC who were killed:

Staff Sergeant David K Ollre (6288183), age 23.

Corporal James A Moore, age 23

Corporal Teddy R Potocki (32141939), age 23

Watson was gazetted on 15 June 1943 with the Distinguished Flying Medal (DFM) for accruing 240 hours operational flying time whilst with RAF 90 Squadron. The recommendation for the medal read: 'The safe return of his aircraft on many occasions must be credited to his skill and knowledge'.

Five of the crew members who survived the crash at Little Glemham – Flight Sergeant Colin George Nairne, Pilot Officer Lyndon Clifford Perry, Sergeant Alfred Richard Stannard, Sergeant Stanley Alfred George Woodford – were tragically killed just three months later (30 July 1944). They were flying northwards over the English Channel in heavy low cloud on Lancaster Mk.I, HK558, AA-D (RAF 75 Squadron) when they collided with RAF 514 squadron Avro Lancaster, LL733. All the crews from both aircraft were lost. Pilot Officer Frederick Gerald Rickard was the only one to live through the war – he died in 1998.

Watson was the eldest son of William and Christina Watson, Isaville, Bankfoot, Perthshire. He is buried in Auchtergaven Parish Churchyard, Perthshire. He is also commemorated on the Auchtergaven War Memorial. A military funeral was accorded to Warrant Officer William (Sandy) Alexander Watson. In attendance were contingents of the RAF, Home Guard, and the Observer Corps along with many of the public. The coffin was draped in the Union Flag and was carried from the house to the churchyard by each of the services representatives. A salute of guns was fired at the graveside and a bugler sounded 'The Last Post'.

Notes:

Lady MacRobert also sponsored four Hawker Hurricanes, three named after her sons and the fourth honouring the fighting spirit of the Russian allies carried the inscription, 'MacRobert's Salute to Russia'. Through the years many RAF aircraft have been given the names 'MacRobert's Reply': a Hawker Siddeley Buccaneer and four Panavia Tornados. Her sons, Sir Iain, Sir Roderic and Sir Alasdair have had nine RAF aircraft named after them.

A second Short Stirling, 'MacRobert's Reply' (W7531) entered service in March 1942 and was lost on 18 May 1942, only one member of the crew survived. W7531 was carrying out a 'Gardening Daffodil' operation off the Danish coast, laying mines to sink enemy shipping. Take off was from RAF Wyton at 21.40 hours. On approaching the south entrance to Øresund via the Norwegian coast and Malmo, the Short Stirling dropped down to 200 feet as they closed in on their target area. The aircraft was sudenly lit up by the searchlights of their old adversary, the Hipper Class cruiser, Prinz Eugen. The Prinz Eugen had just survived the Channel Dash and was now heading towards the Kiel Canal. The cruiser opened up with anti-aircraft, scoring numerous hits, while her escorts and shore batteries also struck the Stirling with machine gun and anti-aircraft fire.

W7531 was badly damaged, and fires broke out, the pilot Squadron Leader John Hall DFC turned west and tried to guide the Stirling to open water, but anti-aircraft posts (3.lei Flak Abt. 844 II and IV Zugdealt) on the nearby Lille Bælt Bridge hit the aircraft several times with flak. The Short Stirling crashed at 02.10 hours into the Gals Klint forest, approximately 2 km to the west of Middelfart. When the Short Stirling hit the ground, one of the remaining mines onboard exploded and the plane was totally wrecked.

Among that blazing wreckage something stirred, it was Sergeant Donald Jeffs, although severly wounded, he would the only one to survive. Jeffs was taken by the Wehrmacht to the lazarett (hospital) in Fredericia, and later to the lazarett in Rendsburg. When he had recovered from his wounds, he was sent on to Stalag VIIIB / 344 Lamsdorf. After the war, a memorial stone was raised on the spot where W7531 crashed and every year on 5 May, the day of the liberation of Denmark, a ceremony is held at the site.

Grafton Underwood was the fictional childhood home of Bridget Jones in the novels by Helen Fielding, Bridget Jones Diary. During the Second World War, RAF Grafton Underwood was assigned to the USAF Eighth Air Force in 1942 as USAAF Station 106.

RAF Polebrook was the airfield from which the USAF's Eighth Air Force carried out its first heavy bomb group combat mission on 17 August 1942. Major Clark Gable the film star flew combat missions from here in 1943.

MACROBERT'S REPLY (CH 3945) Original wartime caption: 'MACROBERT'S REPLY' the bomber aircraft purchased by Lady MacRobert and presented to the R.A.F. in memory of her sons - is now in operation with Bomber Command and has already taken part in raids on enemy territory. The Wing Commander [W/Cdr.Ogilvie] commanding the squadron with which 'MacRobert's Reply' is operating, handing to the crew a letter from Lady MacRobert, wishi... Copyright: © IWM. Original Source: http://www.iwm.org.uk/collections/item/object/205444707

'MacROBERT'S REPLY? (CH 3231) Original wartime caption: A recent portrait of Lady MacRobert. Copyright: © IWM. Original Source: http://www.iwm.org.uk/collections/item/object/205444123

BILL PRUNE: MASCOT OF AN R.A.F. BOMBER SQUADRON: R.I.P. (CH 12815) Original wartime caption: Flight Lieutenant William Prune, bulldog mascot of a bomber squadron stationed in East Anglia, is dead. Born on 23rd May 1938 and named Bill of Bafford, he first served with an Army Unit. Bill granted a commission in the R.A.F.V.R. and, on 11th March 1942 posted to a bomber squadron for operational duties as a Pilot Officer. He immediately established himself as a firm fa... Copyright: © IWM. Original Source: http://www.iwm.org.uk/collections/item/object/20545237

In memory of William Prune of RAF 15 Squadron, he had his own logbook and undertook at least 14 flights, no one though, would ever claim to have taken him aloft. His favourite pastime was chasing motorcycles, attempting to bite the front tyre. His career ended when he attempted to do this with a lorry.

IWM PST 14973

"We'll do our job - -if you'll do yours"

The crew of the bomber plane "MacRobert's Reply" all ready to take off for a raid over enemy territory

We'll Do Our Job - If You'll Do Yours (Art.IWM PST 14973) whole: the image occupies the majority, with the title integrated and placed in the upper right, in black. The text is
separate and positioned across the bottom edge, also in black, set against a white background.
image: a photograph of the six crew members of the British Short Stirling bomber aircraft 'MacRobert's Reply'. As they line up to board
their aircraft, they laugh and joke with each othe... Copyright: © IWM. Original Source:
http://www.iwm.org.uk/collections/item/object/32405

18 Bourne End Rail Crash

Perhaps the most tragic event to befall the people of this area happened just one month after the end of World War Two. The rail crash in 1979 at Invergowrie was not the worst to affect the people of Perth and Perthshire. Bourne End was truly tragic, newlyweds, soldiers being de-mobbed, just released POW's, many had served in combat and not been home for years. To them, it was all over, and they were looking forward to life returning to peaceful and happy normalcy.

On the night of 30 September 1945, the overnight train to London Euston Station left Perth packed with over 700 people on board, many of them servicemen and women. It was a 15-coach express train hauled by The London, Midland and Scotland, Royal Scot Class 4-6-0 No. 6157, The Royal Artilleryman. Due to engineering work being carried out on the Watford Tunnel, the train was diverted from the fast lanes to the slow lanes at Bourne End, near Hemel Hempstead in the Borough of Dacorum. The morning was fine and sunny, and the train driver was highly experienced.

At 8.20pm the driver of the train failed to slow down in response to the cautionary signals on the approach to the diversion. The train entered the 15 miles an hour section at nearly 60 miles per hour. The train derailed and the first 6 carriages overturned and fell down an embankment. Only the last three carriages remained on the rails.

The alarm was raised by a U.S.A.A.F. pilot, Captain McCallum who had just taken off from Bovingdon Aerodrome and observed the accident. He notified his control tower, and they notified the railway authorities. American personal at the aerodrome and local people helped significantly with assistance to the injured. Medical aid was forthcoming at once, a doctor who was a passenger rendered immediate assistance and was joined by another doctor at 9.20pm and two more at 9.30pm. The first casualty was admitted to the West Hertfordshire Hospital, three miles away at 9.30pm.

Local St. John's ambulance crews arrived at the horrific crash within 20 minutes and were soon joined by ambulances from further afield. The residents of the hamlet of Bourne End were having a VJ (Victory over Japan) party as the train derailed. The uneaten sandwiches and sausage rolls were welcomed by the survivors. The Berkhamsted Woman's Voluntary Service quickly provided urns of hot tea.

The first carriage, a luggage van was completely crushed by the second carriage and flung at right angles above it. The floor of the third carriage was ripped out and it was left pointing into the air at 45 degrees. The fourth carriage lay alongside the third.

43 people were killed and 124 injured, 64 seriously. Among the dead and injured were members of the Services who had fought on many battlefields and had just returned from the war safely.

Perthshire Casualties:

Former Leading Aircraftwoman Lillian Mary Bennett Edwards, 462073, Women's Auxiliary Air Force, Age 25. Mrs Lillian Edwards died on 1st October 1945 at the West Hertfordshire Hospital. Lilian was stationed at RAF Leuchars until her demobilisation three weeks previously. A guard of honour of W.A.A.F.'s from

Leuchars escorted the hearse from her parents' home at 11 Park Crescent, Scone to Scone Cemetery. Helen was travelling with her new husband, Corporal Leslie Edwards from Coulson in Surrey. He was uninjured in the crash.

Corporal Helen Ann Taylor (Nicky) Grassie, W/156152, Auxiliary Territorial Service (ATS), age 24. Helen was the daughter of Captain J.T. Grassie, D.S.O., M.B.E., Sports Master at Perth Academy and formerly of the Black Watch, and Mrs Grassie of Atholl Bank Cottage in Perth. Helen was formerly employed in the art department of Munro Press Ltd., Perth.

Sergeant David MacBeth, Black Watch, Age 29 son of Mr George MacBeth, Blackford Estate.

Sergeant William Lumgair, Black Watch, Age 40, formerly a piping instructor at Glenalmond College and a well-known soccer referee and swimmer.

Trooper William Albert Toy, 316888, Royal Armoured Corps, Age 34. His wife lived at 8 Crieff Road, Perth. Trooper Toy was wounded twice in North African and Italian campaigns.

Guardsman Alexander Lachlan Bruce, 2699533, Scots Guards, Age Unknown. Guardsman Bruce was from the Central Hotel in Errol. He was on compassionate leave to attend to the business of his father-in-law who was seriously ill. Guardsman Bruce is buried in Murie Cemetery, Errol.

Leading Aircraftman Henry Albert Frost, 1611304, RAFVR, Age 42, stationed at RAF Errol.

Leading Aircraftman Harry Albert Harris, 1216387, RAFVR, Age 37, stationed at RAF Errol.

Gunner John Smith, 1562772, Royal Artillery, age 32, son of Mary Smith, 31 Darnhall Drive, Craigie, Perth. Gunner Smith was to report to The Royal Arsenal at Woolwich after having served in Italy.

The Perthshire Injured:

Wren Rose Donaldson, age 18 from Ainslie Gardens, Perth.

Wren Catherine West, age 22 from Charlotte Street, Perth

David Grieve, Ainslie Gardens, Perth

Wing Commander Robert Napier, Burnbank Terrace, Perth

David Phillips and Mrs Phillips, George Street, Perth

Chief Petty Officer Douglas Clark, age 29, was going south to take part in a course.

Driver David Birrell, Ballantine Place, Perth was a P.O.W. in Germany for five years and was on his way to re-join his unit.

Able Seaman David Guthrie, Abbot Street, Perth, on route to Plymouth.

Private Alex Miles, age 26, Park Terrace, Perth. Served three years in the Middle East and was returning home after his first leave home in four years.

Thomas Ferrell, 13 George Street, Dunblane.

George Strathdee, 72 George Street, Dunblane.

William, Mrs Betty and Miss Betty Munro, Invergowrie

Lance Corporal Sadgrove, Rosebank, Bankfoot.

Private David Philp, Lance Corporal Ronald Seagrave, Private Peter Francis McFarlane and Corporal James Meek, all stationed at the Queen's Barracks, Perth.

Perthshire Uninjured:

Lieutenant Colonel A. V. Holt, Guildtown.

Buchanan Dunsmore, Comely Bank, Perth.

Flight Lieutenant W. G. Wood, MurrayVille, Kinnoull, Perth.

Eddie Robertson, Black Watch, Ainslie Place, Perth.

Images credit: The Dacorum Heritage Trust Ltd

19 Second Lieutenant Herrick Peter Gladstone Leyden and Second Lieutenant Robert William Gladstone Leyden

Lieutenant Herrick Peter Gladstone Leyden was the son of Patrick Peter and Margaret Florence Gladstone Leyden, of Beechwood, 9 Pitcullen Terrace, Perth. Herrick was born on 24 March 1898 at Pontardawe in the Swansea Valley. His father was a Customs and Excise and Old Age Pensions Officer in Tay Street. He attended Swansea Grammar (Bishop Gore Grammar) from September 1912 to July 1915, Sharp's Institution in South Methven Street and Perth Academy from September 1915 to June 1916.

Herrick who was employed as a motor driver, enlisted in The Black Watch, 3rd Battalion (Royal Highlanders), on 10 January 1917 he signed his service paper, he was aged 18 years and 10 months. Herrick went to The Black Watch army camp at Nigg, Ross-shire for six weeks training and then joined the Royal Flying Corp, 7 March 1917. As a trained flying officer pilot, he went on the RFC list on 5 July 1917. He was promoted on 31 March 1918 on the understanding it was to be confirmed. It was made effective the following day; 1 April 1917 and he was officially gazetted as 2nd Lieutenant on 2 May 1918.

He was again gazetted on 26 July 1917 as Lieutenant, but his CWG (Commonwealth War Graves) entry shows him at time of death as still a 2nd Lieutenant.

His pilot training took him first to:

Officers Cadet Wing at Denham Aerodrome on 8 March 1917.

No. 2 School of Military Aeronautics at Oxford on 11 May 1917.

39 T S (Training Squadron) on 5 July 1917 at Montrose (Note: 39 T.S. is recorded as not coming into operation until 26 August 1917).

61 T S (Training Squadron) of 23 Wing on 20 September 1917 at Cramlington.

51 T S 27 Wing at Filton.

36 T S on 31 October 1917 at Beverley.

58 Squadron, 19th Wing on 8 November 1917 at Cramlington.

75 T S on 28 November 1917 at Waddington. Possibly just for further instruction and returned to 58 Squadron.

No.1 School of Flying and Gunnery at Turnberry on 13 June 1918. Three-week course in the art of aerial gunnery and combat.

Herrick Leyden, age 20, was told he was to be operational in France with 104 Squadron on 28 June 1918, effective 6 July 1918. However, it is possible that he was already posted to France; 58 Squadron departed Dover on 22 December 1917, were based at St Omer, Trézennes, Clairmarais, Auchel, Fauquembergues and Alquines through the first half of 1918.

These airfields would have been covering the battlefields in the Nord-Pas De Calais area during the German Spring Offensives of 1918. As the allies were pushed back, they would have moved back west from 23 April 1918 and through the summer to Fauquembergues and Alquines.

He may have been held in reserve, still under training in England, or was perhaps rested. He could have returned for further gunnery training at Turnberry and was then re-assigned to 104 Squadron who were at Azelot near Nancy.

On 13 August 1918, he was piloting a Geoffrey de Havilland designed Airco DH. 9, single engine, two seat, biplane bomber. The aircraft designation, D7229 was seen to be hit by anti-aircraft fire, fold up and his aircraft fall on to another DH.9, crewed by pilot, 2nd Lieutenant Francis Henry Beaufort (from New York) and Observer, 2nd Lieutenant H O Bryant.

On his RAF Casualty Card, Herrick was reported missing the next day, along with his observer, Sergeant Alan Lacey Windridge age 20, and the two other airmen.

Herrick's Casualty Card and his service records sheets contain other information. A letter was sent on 20 August 1918, to his next of kin, which was listed as his father, informing him that Herrick was missing. There is a pencil note saying that Herrick was buried in a church cemetery and another that he was reported as possibly having crashed at Arnaville. A memo from the Imperial War Graves Commission on 5 March 1921 confirms that he was initially buried close-by in the nearby Array Churchyard, Lorraine – Grave 4.

Arnaville would have been in German held hands at the time, the frontline was near Pont-à-Mousson just to the south, on the Moselle River. His squadron was based at Azelot, about 60 km from Arnaville, again to the south, just below Nancy.

Herrick's bereaved father later received a letter from Major J C Quinell, the officer commanding RAF 104 Squadron in which he referred to Lieutenant Leyden as 'a most excellent officer who did splendid work and would have made a name for himself in the Royal Air Force. Please accept on behalf of his fellow-officers with the squadron my deepest sympathy in your loss'.

Another note on Herrick's Casualty Card states that 'according to inf. from German Red X this officer was killed on 13 August, buried at Ehrenfriedersdorf'. This is most probably a mis-identification error, an Airco DH.9a had the range to reach Ehrenfriedersdorf but would not have the fuel to fly back. Ehrenfriedersdorf is approximately 650Km east of Azelot.

The list of aircraft flown by Herrick Leyden from his service record:

Farman S11 Shorthorn (MF S.H.)

Armstrong Whitworth (possibly a F.K.3)

Royal Aircraft Factory B.E. (possibly a B.E.2)

Airco DH.6

Royal Aircraft Factory R.E.8

Airco DH.9

After the war, Second Lieutenant Leyden and the other three who died were reinterred and buried together in one grave at the Perreuse Chateau, Franco British National Cemetery, 60 km east of Paris. Leyden is commemorated on the war memorials of Perth Academy and the St John the Baptist RC Church, Melville Street, Perth, and on the Bishop Gore School War Memorial, Sketty, West Glamorgan.

Robert William Gladstone Leyden, born 21 April 1900, followed his brother into the RAF. He joined on 8 April 1918 after being declared fit as pilot. There is a note to say that he transferred from Army School to 32 TDS (Training Depot Squadron) at RAF Montrose, RAF 20 Group, effective 14 September 1918. This was less than two months from the end of the war. He was sent to Edinburgh Castle for dispersal back to civilian life on 4 January 1919.

Notes:

The de Havilland Airco DH.9 was first flown in July 1917. They suffered heavy losses due to their unreliability and the poor performance of the 230 hp Armstrong Siddeley Puma 6-cylinder engine. Alternative engines were sought and eventually the US 400hp V-12 Liberty engine was adopted and a redesigned aircraft, the DH.9a was put into service.

During the Great War, 3,024 DH.9s and 2,300 DH.9as were built. They were armed with a forward firing Vickers machine gun and one or two rear firing Lewis guns on a Scarf ring. The DH.9as could carry up to 740 lb of bombs under the wings and on fuselage racks.

RAF 104 Squadron was formed on 4 September 1917 at Wyton, England. It moved to Andover and then to France in May 1918. When the war ended, the Squadron returned home, first to RAF Turnhouse, Edinburgh and was disbanded on 30 June 1919, at RAF Crail, Fife. 104 Squadron was part of the Independent Force (RAF) of the British Expeditionary Force (BEF). The Independent Air Force (IAF) was a First World War strategic bombing force which was part of the RFC/RAF that could strike against German railways, aerodromes, and industrial centres without co-ordination with the Army or Navy.

Also on 13 August 1918, USAF Pilot, Field Eugene Kindley shot down Lothar von Richthofen, the brother of the late great German war ace Manfred von Richthofen. Lothar had 40 confirmed air-to-air victories at the time, he suffered serious wounds when he crashed and never flew in combat again.

RAF Turnberry was used for the testing of Barnes Wallis's 'Highball' bouncing bombs by RAF 618 squadron during the Second World War. An old French Battleship, the Courbet and later the HMS Malaya were anchored in Loch Striven (above Rothesay) and were used as practice targets for the bouncing bombs. The loch was also used for the training of X-craft midget submarines. Both these weapons were to be used against the German Battleship Tirpitz, anchored in a Norwegian Fjord. The Tirpitz was later sunk on 12 November 1944 by Avro Lancaster bombers using the also designed by Barnes Wallis 'Tallboy"' bombs.

The day before Herrick Leyden was killed marked the end of the Battle of Amiens (8-12 August 1918), and the start of the Allied counteroffensive known as the 'Hundred Days Offensive'. This led to the end of the war with the Armistice being signed in a railroad carriage at Compiègne on 11 November 1918. It had all started on 21 March 1918 with the last effort, the 'German Spring Offensives', a series of large-scale surprise attacks against the Allied lines along the mostly northern length of the Western Front. By the end of August 1918, the Germans had been driven back and greatly weakened by the loss of men and morale.

At 11 am on 11 November 1918 – 'the eleventh hour of the eleventh day of the eleventh month' – a ceasefire came into effect.

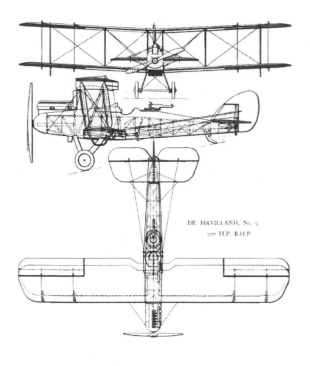

DE HAVILLAND, No. 9.
200 H.P. B.H.P.

Image courtesy of the Perth Academy Flowers of the Forest First World War commemorative project
Herrick Leyden, 2nd from left, middle row
William Soutar (Poet) 1st on left, front row

ABOUT THE AUTHOR

Ken Bruce was born in Cluny Terrace in the Letham area of Perth. Educated at Carntyne Primary (Glasgow), Letham Primary, Goodlyburn Junior Secondary, Perth High School (Muirton), Perth College of Further Education and the Open University.

After retirement, Ken began researching several local history topics, specialising in aviation and military history.

Author of **Where Sky and Summit Meet**, published by Tippermuir Books Ltd. Perth
Available from: **Tippermuirbooks.co.uk**

Researcher and writer of local aviation and military history stories on the website: **madeinperth.org**

Author - Age 20

Printed in Great Britain
by Amazon

79497939R00079